A Lakeland Boyhood

The author with Ozzy, 2019.

A Lakeland Boyhood

DAVID CLARK

(Lord Clark of Windermere)

HAYLOFT

Published by Hayloft Publishing Ltd., 2020

A CIP catalogue record for this book is available from the British Library

ISBN 978-1-910237-61-8

Designed, printed and bound in the UK and EU

Hayloft policy is to use papers that are natural, renewable and recyclable products and made from wood grown in sustainable forests. The logging and manufacturing processes are expected to conform to the environmental regulations of the country of origin.

Climate neutral
Print product
ClimatePartner.com/12667-2004-1003

This book was printed with the offset of carbon emissions
and support for forest protection in Pará, Brazil

Hayloft Publishing Ltd,
a company registered in England number 4802586
10 Kendal Fell Business Park, Kendal, LA9 5RR (registered office)
L'Ancien Presbytère, 21460 Corsaint, France (editorial office)

Email: books@hayloft.eu
Tel: 07971 352473
www.hayloft.eu

Cover photograph view of Windermere from Rosthwaite Lot.

To my parents whose story this is too.
Their beliefs and determination made it possible.

Also by David Clark

The Industrial Manager

Colne Valley: Radicalism to Socialism

Victor Grayson: Labour's Lost Leader

We Do No Want the Earth:
The history of South Shields Labour Party

The Labour Movement in Westmorland

Voices from Labour's Past

Victor Grayson: The Man and the Mystery

Contents

Foreword

"A sort of national property in which every man has a right and interest who has an eye to perceive and a heart to enjoy"
William Wordsworth

The Lake District is a wonderful place to live as well as visit. Only just over forty thousand of us are residents and we welcome nineteen million visitors each year who come to enjoy its beauty. We understand why they come, after all we have chosen to live here. Its appeal is universal.

However, it wasn't always viewed in this light. Before Wordsworth, Daniel Defoe in his tour of Britain between 1724-6, described the area as, "...the wildest, most barren and frightful of any that I have passed over in England."

Since then opinions have changed as has the landscape itself – at the hands of man. The reality is that the beauty of Lakeland is shaped by nature and then moulded by human activities. The sheep and cattle farmers of the uplands cleared the scrub trees and opened up the fells to grazing, providing humans with inspirational views and the freedom to roam at will. The traditional sheep breed, the Herdwicks are 'hefted' to the land and won't stray from it.

This mountainous area has been mined for over a thousand years. There have been over 1,000 mines and quarries, with more than twenty minerals being extracted. The tourist hot-spot of Coniston has its extensive copper mines whilst Grasmere and Glenridding have also the remains of lead mines.

In the valleys, farming and woodland existed side by side. The woods were coppiced and pollarded, providing the raw material for the local bobbin mills. These more lowland farms were mixed. Dairy, sheep and a little arable proved to be successful almost to the end of the twentieth century whilst at the same time providing an aesthetically attractive countryside to locals and visitors alike. This upland and valley landscape is the basis of the area's attraction to visitors.

In 1951, the area became England's largest national park. Then the final accolade came in 2017 when UNESCO decided the Lake District was worthy of joining the elite group of World Heritage

Sites. This international accolade has taken over thirty years of effort to achieve and I was honoured to have led the campaign for the final ten.

UNESCO were very clear that the reason for the designation was the area's exceptional 'cultural landscape' – 'Centuries of interaction between nature and activities of local communities, visitors and industry characterise the cultural landscape of the Lake District.'

This book is about growing up in the post war years of austerity. It is about the village where I was brought up, went to school and began my working life in the 1940s and 1950s. My memories of Bowness are that of a thriving, living community. It was a happy place in which to live with a great deal of life going on. Since then, it has changed beyond recognition. Change is of course inevitable. This has to be accepted but not all change is for the best. World Heritage Site Status is based on man enhancing an environment and society. Both must be in balance. The massive growth in tourism has swamped a local community. Thought needs to be given and action taken to ensure this never happens again.

This book is about my life and the place where I grew up. I have discussed life in the village of Bowness with others who lived there in the same period, but what is written is mine alone. They are my thoughts and opinions.

In particular, I would like to thank the following who generously shared their memories and experiences with me: John Beckett, Gerald Brear, Ernie Fallowfield, Frank Hantom, Derek Hewitson, John Hiley, Joyce Hoggarth, Peter Hoggarth, Mel Jeffrey, Iain Johnston, Peter and Susan Lever, John and Pat McDougall, David and Margaret Richardson, Roy Shorrock, David Telford Reed, Colin and Margaret Tyson. They all gave their time willingly and provided me with much information and encouragement. They have been my friends for many years and I trust nothing in this book will change that. I value their friendship.

I have also made new friends. In particular, Ian Gee and David Harrigan spent much time in outlining the early flying initiatives on Windermere. Their efforts in keeping the story of *Waterbird* through the Lakes Flying Company deserves success. The Rector, the Revd James Richards, has provided much new information for which I am most grateful. I thank them all, as well as many others who helped me along the way. At the end of the day however, the memories, opinions and thoughts are mine. I accept full responsibility for them.

1
The Beginning

When I say I was born in a stable, many immediately jump to the conclusion that I am suffering delusions of grandeur. But I'm not, for I shared my birthplace with horses and a sawmill. The stable block still stands, with the physical shape of the building having changed little over time. The National Trust for Scotland has acquired the estate and turned the stables and sawmill into a rather bijou café and toilets. The two cottages remain but, thankfully, much improved and slightly extended, yet still exceedingly small.

It was during the early months of the Second World War, on 19 October 1939, that I first saw the light of day in this small cottage without electricity and with water drawn from an outside pump. My father, George Clark, was the head gardener employed by Major Alan Gordon of Threave House, a mile or so distance from the market town of Castle Douglas in the Stewarty of Kirkcudbright.

We shared our accommodation with the animals and my father

Threave Cottage where the author was born.

1

always maintaining his employers cared more for the horses than they did for their workers. Perhaps this was exemplified in his diary entry of the day of my birth which simply recorded 'picked last of the apples'.

He prided himself on his profession as a gardener. He had served his apprenticeship at Lowther Castle in Westmorland which was reputed as having one of the most extensive gardens in England owned by the infamous 5th Earl of Lonsdale, the 'Yellow Earl'.

His Lordship was a larger than life character who managed to gamble away most of the immense family fortune. The Lonsdales owned much of what is now Cumbria in addition to having properties and homes throughout the United Kingdom. The Earl loved the 'good life', his London parties were legendary, whilst his name lives on as the result of his having donated the famous Lonsdale Belts to the boxing world. He had a penchant for the colour yellow. All his coaches were yellow as were later his many Rolls Royces whilst even his gundogs were golden (yellow) labradors.

He was a close friend of the Kaiser, a member of the German Royal Household and an outspoken supporter of the German military machine. When the First World War broke out he was viewed with great suspicion by the British military establishment. Although in time he became a considerable donor to the allied war effort including the financing of the Lonsdale Battalion of the Border Regiment. My father recalled that locally it was widely known that pressure was put on his Lordship by the authorities not to travel far from his Lowther Estate. The result was that he spent much of the war working in his extensive gardens. During these years my father, as a young apprentice, worked alongside him but was always somewhat sceptical of his gardening skills.

The Lonsdales were strongly anti-socialist. This however did not stop the young gardener becoming one of the founder members in 1918 of the local trade union branch of the Agricultural Workers Union, an action which undoubtedly horrified 'Lordie' as my father always called him. Dad told me that when he was quite young, he had come under the influence of the local vicar at Askham and Lowther Churches, the Rev W B Graham. The vicar had sided with the land workers from the day of his appointment, actively encouraging and supporting them to form a local trade union branch. He radicalised my father who was nearing the end of his apprenticeship and took the risk of joining the union. He was impressed by the vicar whom he described as, "As a gert lang fella (a great tall man) who couldn't half talk."

Many years later, I wrote a biography of Victor Grayson MP, who had won a spectacular parliamentary by-election for Colne Valley in 1907 and for a few years was the terror of the British establishment being seen as possibly bringing about a revolution in the country. One of his key supporters was a young curate in the constituency called W B Graham who was a brilliant orator. He was six feet five inches tall and I recognised him as the same vicar who had so impressed my Dad. My father did not get many prizes at school but he did from W B Graham at Sunday School. That may be some indication of his regard for the vicar. It is a mystery why Lord Lonsdale had appointed him as the local vicar in view of his widely known political views, but he did.

Between 1766-73, Sir James Lowther later Lord Lonsdale, in order to improve the vista from his castle cleared the houses where his employees lived and appointed Robert Adam to design a model village. In 1968 the village was declared a Grade II listed building. It is certainly an unusual set of houses which could easily be mistaken for army barracks. My grandfather who worked on the estate lived there and thus my father, George, was born in one of those cottages. As an aside, it is somewhat ironic that in the 21st century, the Lonsdales, who trace their origins back centuries, are not represented in the House of Lords yet the son of one of their gardeners is.

My mother Janet had Cumbrian roots too. Her father was a coal miner in County Durham as was his father who had been born in Cumbria and began his working life as a miner near Brampton in the East Cumberland coalfield. The mines there were in decline and he moved across the Pennines to where there was plenty of work in the newer pits of Durham.

Therefore, coming as my father did from this long line of Cumbrians, it is something of a mystery that twenty years later he appears as head gardener at Threave on 30 December 1938. The surviving records of Threave Estate show that he was paid forty shillings a week plus unemployment and health insurance.

Prior to this he seemed to have been happily employed for almost ten years in the gardens of Lindeth Fell, Windermere. On 4 July 1931, he had married my mother Janet who hailed from Sunderland and been working in service as a housemaid in one of the many big houses around Windermere. However, they had lost an older son, my brother Ian, who had died and the wish to ease the pain of that sad event may explain their move to Scotland. Perhaps one consolation was that the mountains of Cumbria which they both loved were visible from the higher parts of Threave Gardens.

Obviously as a young child, my memories of life at Threave are somewhat vague but I do remember playing with gundogs whose kennels were only a few yards from where we lived and even have photographs of me straddling a retriever dog which was bigger than myself. I can still recall sitting by the flower beds picking the purple heads off *Primula Denticulata* flowers whilst soldiers rode past on their horses.

Living adjacent to us was Mrs Moore and her four children in terribly overcrowded conditions. Her husband had been Major Alan Gordon's batman in the Irish Guards during the First World War and was away in the army during the second conflict. The youngest daughter Patricia confirms that there were soldiers about the grounds and remembers her older sister recounting that one of them had made dubious passes at her which had been reported to my father who 'sorted the matter out'. There is a photograph of my father in army uniform where he is apparently standing alone. Interestingly, I discovered this photograph had been cut off a larger one. From the shadows in the original photograph of Dad, it could easily be discerned that he had been in a line of soldiers standing at ease. Whatever activities he was involved in, he had the use of a motor vehicle in which he travelled around Galloway giving talks and lectures but on what subjects remains unclear.

There were two Gordon brothers, both with military backgrounds, who ran the Threave Estate. The older, Major Colin had served in the Coldstream Guards and died in August 1940. Major Alan briefly took over the sole responsibility for running the estate before the property was requisitioned by the War Office. In 1948 he donated the house and estate to the National Trust for Scotland and lived in the house until his death in November 1957. The gardens were opened to the public and I always enjoyed returning to my earliest haunts on visits to Galloway.

Then in 2002 the 'Big House' was opened for short tours and I was lucky enough to join one of these. In each of the principal downstairs rooms I noticed that there were buff-coloured folders on the tables and sideboards. I flicked one open and saw that under the heading of Ministry of War was a list of items in the room which had been requisitioned in the early months of Second World War. I took a peep into the folders in each room and found similar lists.

Throughout the conducted tour, the guide made no mention of the war years. At the end I quietly inquired of her what had been the army's activities on the estate during the war. She vehemently denied there had been any. To her embarrassment, I showed her one of the War Office requisitioning folders from one of the rooms and then to make my point, mentioned that I had lived on the estate during the early 1940s and that there had been many soldiers around. The conversation ended with the frustrated guide admitting that she had been instructed by her superiors to always deny point blank that there had been any military presence whatsoever on the estate but she knew no more than that. I thought that strange.

Why the secrecy sixty years after the war had ended? I wrote to the National Trust for Scotland where the archivist made a thorough investigation into my request for information. He searched all the records of Threave and discovered a full set with the exception of the war years which inexplicably were missing. Interestingly in 2017, I made a further tour of the house when I found that the War Office requisitioning folders had disappeared.

Author sitting on the gun dog, aged 21 months, 1941.

Events however, overtook our family when we moved a dozen or so miles to the Solway coast near Kirkbean. The children's charity Barnardo's had taken over the estate of the Blacketts at Arbigland for the duration of the war and my father had been installed as head gardener with instructions to produce sufficient food for the evacuated children with any surplus being sent to Dumfries Station for onward transmission to assist the war effort nationally. This was in 1943/4 when I was storing up more clearer memories.

The tied house into which we moved was once more very basic indeed. No electricity and with the inevitable toilet or privy at the bottom of the garden. Our lighting was provided by candles or oil lamps and we somehow acquired a Tilly Lamp that needed much pumping to get it going but which then provided an excellent light. If I concentrate very hard I can still hear the hissing of that lamp. Heating was by logs from the surrounding woods and cooking by means of an oil stove or the kitchen fire. Our wireless, powered by battery, was the only contact with the outside world and of knowing how the war was going. The batteries were thick glass containers filled with acid. As they ran down, the acid needed re-charging which meant the whole battery had to be carried down to the village shop. These were exceedingly heavy so as a young boy it was left to my mother to struggle with them.

Our new home was only a field away from the shore of the Solway Firth with an open prospect across the firth to the town of Silloth in England, ten miles distance and with the Cumbrian Mountains dominating the horizon. Very quickly this became heaven to me especially when I discovered a boy of my age, Ronnie Duggan, living only a hundred yards or so down the lane. Together we explored every inch of the shoreline with its rocky outcrops, sandy beaches and best of all, caves. It didn't take much to imagine these being used by pirates and smugglers in past days.

Our fantasies were heightened when we discovered a local hero, John Paul Jones. That he was born in one of the gardeners' cottages on the estate on 6 July 1747, fuelled our imagination further. Jones had served in the British Navy but when the American War of Independence began he switched sides and is widely accepted as the 'founder of the US Navy'. Using his knowledge of the coast, in April 1778 Jones raided the port of Whitehaven across the Solway in Cumbria, causing terror before going on to create near panic with further raids on the east coast of England the following year. He

George and Janet Clark with their son David.

was honoured by the French and in 1782 enlisted in the Russian Navy as a rear admiral. Not surprisingly he became the inspiring hero for we two young explorers. As recognition of his changing sides so often, he is more widely remembered by having a popular dance, involving a regular change of partners, named after him.

Putting our hero to one side, we continued with our own exploration. When the tide receded, the remaining shallow pools of water often contained stranded flukes or flounders which we became very adept at catching. This involved identifying the most likely pools and then gently inserting my fingers to feel for the fish before flipping it out of its watery refuge. They regularly featured on the family dinner plates.

We searched the rocks for gulls' nests but we only took eggs home once with the view of supplementing our meals. We got short shrift for our troubles with a stern telling-off for bringing these 'awful fishy tasting eggs home'. We never repeated the gesture. In any case the gulls laid their eggs in spring when there was an abundance of hens' eggs. We kept hens and if we had a glut of eggs during the summer months with their long daylight hours, my parents carefully preserved them. They bought sodium silicate powder which was mixed with water in a metal bucket with a lid. The eggs were not washed but their shells were cleaned with a dry cloth and then carefully placed in the solution. There they would remain until needed. The eggs would easily be safely preserved for up to six months. Throughout the war, we were fortunate in having an adequate supply of eggs all year round.

An additional help in our efforts at self-sufficiency, or at least making us less dependent on wartime rationing, were the bees my father kept. He had several hives and he treated the bees as his pets. I can still see him with a veil covering his face and holding a smoking set of portable bellows which he used to subdue the bees when he was working inside the hives. In spite of the hundreds of bees around him, I can't ever recall him getting stung. I also remember the excitement when the bees swarmed. He collected them with

Trying a pipe with his Dad!

great care before installing them into an empty hive. This helped us to have a supply of honey for most of the year.

The Government were so keen for people to keep bees that an extra sugar supply was available to bee-keepers to ensure that the bees survived the winter months. This was critical for all the honey the bees had made during the summer to keep them going throughout the winter months, had been removed to assist in the war effort. My mother would surreptitiously use a little of the 'bees' sugar to make jam, which she justified as helping the fight against Hitler.

Another major life change took place when the time came for me to start school. This entailed travelling to the local primary school in Kirkbean, the nearest village which was two miles from home. Initially I made the journey on a three-wheeled bike before quickly graduating to a two-wheeler. It was a revelation to meet all the other boys and girls of my own age and I quickly adapted and thoroughly enjoyed the experience. The school was typical of its day in Scotland; strong discipline enforced by the liberal use of the strap. Being a talkative child, I was regularly disciplined by the teacher giving me the strap on my hand.

We were, by and large, a healthy group. Ironically, the wartime rationing ensured everyone had access to at least a supply of basic food. We were all very skinny but at the same time very healthy. The children at Kirkbean School would have been healthier than most for, in addition to the rationing, we had access to much locally produced food. I was no exception. With my father being a gardener, our family had the choice of an even wider selection of food. The climate on the Solway Coast was renowned for its mildness benefitting from the Gulf Stream with the result there was a plethora of fruit. Not only did we benefit from apples and pears but also raspberries, strawberries, peaches and blackberries. In addition, there was a supply of fresh vegetables for almost every month of the year. My father was a first class shot and we regularly had rabbits and wood pigeons on our dinner plates. Small wonder that with all the fresh air and exercise, coupled with a wide variety of local produce, including fish from the sea and local lochs, which enhanced the wartime rationing, we were a healthy generation growing up in the beautiful countryside of South West Scotland.

Of course, it was very much a rural working-class district without any middle-class presence. We were all poor. In summer the children ran around in plimsolls which were called sandshoes whilst in winter our footwear was clogs which were made locally of leather, sycamore wood soles underpinned with iron caulkers. These permitted sparks to fly when one slid along the tarmacadam roads. However, they truly excelled in the snow which stuck to the iron and increased one's height by inches. Such simple pleasures. Black boots if we had them were kept for best.

The author with his best friend Pat, Broad Leys, 1948.

I was an only child having lost the brother I had never known. But I never felt lonely as I always had my friends. Then one day, something happened which was to change my way of life forever. My father came home from work one day with a puppy. The moment I saw and fondled her, I found a soul mate. She was a cross between a golden labrador and a spaniel whom I named Pat. Over time we became virtually inseparable except when I was at school. Even then on my return, she would be waiting at the end of the lane for me. Not for her the need of a clock for she had a built-in timer. She had a lovely nature and together we explored the fields and the shore. I loved her. Since then throughout my life, I have usually had a dog. Every one of them has always given so much and yet expected so little.

But my mother found life in deep rural Scotland difficult; its remoteness, the lack of basic domestic amenities and its reliance on candles and oil lamps. During the war years this was inconvenient but when the blackout curtains were taken down when the war ended in 1945 and the bright lights could be seen in the towns and villages across the Solway in Cumbria, my mother increasingly yearned for electric lights. More than ever, it made her desperate to return to England, although that was not immediately possible for there were still restrictions on movement in relation to jobs. Meanwhile, I was bemused by my mother telling me that one had only to flick a switch for the room to light-up.

2
The Move to England

The winter of 1946/7 was one of the worst on record although it wasn't until the days began to lengthen that the coldest days arrived. It began in January 1947. Between then and March, for 55 consecutive days snow fell somewhere in Britain. Then on March 11 and 12, Scotland bore the brunt with its heaviest snowfalls of the winter with drifts of more than 23 feet deep. Galloway suffered as much as anywhere and I can still recall snow drifts being higher that the telegraph poles, the wires themselves having already been brought down. We were snowed in for days and initially couldn't struggle to our neighbours. Food became extremely short and even we, with our privileged supply, were down to our final scraps.

Every man was expected to help clear the roads including the German and Italian prisoners of war. These men worked on the local farms and gardens alongside the locals and wandered around freely in their spare time. They were already known to us and were generally very kind to children, making us toys out of wood. Many seemed to be accomplished carvers. I guess we reminded them of their own families back home.

Roads were blocked across Britain and trains abandoned. The food situation became worse as lorries carrying food supplies were left stranded. Food was frozen on farms immobilised by snow and ice. Over 70,000 tons of potatoes were destroyed by the cold. Later in the year it became necessary to introduce potato rationing for the first time and the bread ration, which had only been introduced the previous year, was cut even further. The situation was desperate but our limited self-sufficiency meant life at Arbigland was marginally better than for most people.

It was against this unpropitious background that my parents told me that we were moving back to Cumbria. My mother was over the moon that my father had been appointed head gardener at Broad Leys, straddling the boundary between Lancashire and Westmorland, and set on the shores of Windermere. On 7 April 1947, we set-off in a small furniture lorry with our limited belongings in that terrible winter with snow still lining the roadsides. The hard work had been successful and the roads were just about passable for our journey.

My initial impressions of our new home were mixed. The countryside contained more houses than in Scotland but there were plenty of woodlands and fields. The small estate belonged to Frederick John Milne who had retired from the up-market store of Kendal Milnes in Manchester. It didn't take me long to discover a boy of similar age, Gerald Brear, whose father was head gardener at Ghyll Head, a large house only half a mile across two fields. His parents had come to the Lakes from Lancashire and he had a sister who was seven years older than myself but we rarely came in contact with her as she was a nurse in Bolton.

Gerald quickly became a close friend and we spent many hours together roaming the fields, woods and fells. I was told, that during the Second World War, Ghyll Head had been used by the military and the field behind his house contained yards of thin electrical wire of many different bright colours. An old ambulance and double decker bus had been discarded near the narrow road on the edge of the fellside for use by the soldiers, and occasionally by the local home guard unit, for training. They weren't removed after the war and we youngsters spent hours playing in those semi-derelict vehicles.

Our new home was the lodge of a very imposing big house which had been designed by C F A Voysey, one of the most eminent of the Arts and Crafts architects. It had been commissioned in 1898 and completed three years later. It is regarded as one of the three best examples of the Arts and Crafts Movement in the Lake District. It was built there because of the sheer beauty of its position overlooking the lake. The money to build this fine house in its beautiful surroundings had been made in the smoky factories of industrial Yorkshire. Gone was the fussiness of the Victorian age to be replaced by the conceptual simplicity of William Morris and John Ruskin. This simplicity was enhanced by the dignity of labour and natural and outstanding beauty of the setting. The movement was a particular English phenomenon yet utilising the concepts of the pre-industrial age. Broad Leys was a truly beautiful house and remains so.

Our home, the lodge at the entrance of a short drive to the main house, retained the same overall basic style of architecture but with much more local stone exposed. The architectural writer Matthew Hyde in his fine book, *Broad Leys*, wrote, "The lodge is a neat pleasing little house, with sloping buttresses, big square chimneys (the far end has been cut short) and at least one of the original bellied chimneypots. The plan is clever without seeming so. The long rectangular footprint has a corner cut out to make a covered porch. The far end is cross-roofed. The interior is surprising because the floor levels of the cross-roofed part are staggered, with half-flights of stairs up or down from the rest of the house. All the lost spaces under and over stairs are used, nothing is wasted."

The building may look attractive from the outside but due to its smallness wasn't the most convenient to live in. The different levels which evoked architectural plaudits made the house difficult as a dwelling. Whilst the Arts and Crafts philosophy worked well in buildings of size and substance, it wasn't always successful in lesser buildings. A similar contradiction is that the early socialistic advocates of the architecture used expensive traditional skills which ironically ensured that only the very rich could afford them.

The saving grace for my mother was that the house had electricity. She had longed to press a switch and for there to be light. Broad Leys, and its lodge, had electricity installed from the outset. The original owner was Arthur Currer Briggs who, although he had made his fortune from coal mining at Whitwood near Wakefield, was an enthusiast for electricity. The Windermere area was one of the earliest to have electricity but our supply came from the nearby Ghyll Head Reservoir where a generator had been built into the dam at the turn of the century. We were lucky to have a mains supply from the adjacent road. Any difficulties however didn't bother me as I seemed to spend all my days out of doors. The life style I had become used to in Scotland was easily transferred to Broad Leys.

Another reason for my seemingly easy move to England was that I immediately went to a new junior school, Windermere Endowed Boys School, which was in Bowness and had for a period in the nineteenth century been the home of Windermere Grammar School. The school was relatively small with four classes, taught by two teachers. It was an old school building up a steep hill from St Martin's Parish Church. It was a Church of England School which meant the rector was a regular visitor and gave talks to the boys and we attended the church on key dates. Our school's foundation stone had been laid in 1836 by the poet, William Wordsworth, who lived in nearby Grasmere.

The position of the school was on top of a large rocky promon-

Broad Leys Lodge.

tory which had a sheer rocky face of about fifty feet. I'm certain that it would not have been built there today due to the risk to the children. The result however was that the view was one of the most spectacular of any school in Britain. It towered over the old village of Bowness with the church nestling in its centre and with the lake stretching out behind it. The vista across the lake was of Claife Heights with the mountains of Coniston Old Man and Wetherlam in the middle distance. Slightly to the north, the iconic Langdale Pikes were clearly visible with England's highest mountain Scafell Pike a little further away. It was a truly magnificent prospect, one of the finest anywhere.

The school was surrounded by playgrounds on three sides, all of which were extremely stony, far from level and with no grass. We played football with a tennis ball during the breaks but usually our play was on our hands and knees in the stones and dirt making garages and roads for our Dinky toy cars. Ex-army vehicles were still very popular with memories of the war still fresh in our young minds. At an early age we learned how to make 'tanks' out of used cotton bobbins. We inserted a rubber band through the central hole of the bobbin and then attached sliced candles with two used matchsticks at each end. By twisting the matches, the rubber band in turn became twisted and when the bobbin was fully wound it was placed on the ground and moved along. A homemade toy which gave us endless fun. Interestingly the bobbin was probably made in one of the local mills from a birch tree.

Everyone was welcoming and I took to it immediately. I made friends very quickly, some of whom I still see today. I found no difficulty with the schooling for the standard of education in Scotland was good and I was usually somewhere near the top of the class. From my school reports I know that in my first year I was only seventh out of thirteen, by July 1949 I was first before slipping back to fourth in 1950, whilst, as I left school in 1951, I had regained first place. The record of my attendance was consistently described by the headmaster as, 'regular and punctual'. My experience at the school was a key factor in my settling in Bowness. I became happy very quickly.

The school had two teachers, each with a classroom of boys from two different years being taught together and, by skilful handling, following different syllabuses. Our teacher in the lower class, the recently qualified Miss Parkin, introduced new ideas and was loved by all. The facilities might be basic but the tuition was thorough. Occasionally things did go seriously wrong. Two years prior to my taking the eleven plus, David Richardson recalls that in 1949 every one of his class failed the examination which seems statistically unlikely and suggests something went seriously wrong with the teaching in that particular year.

In the lower classroom we used a pencil but in the higher standards, we graduated to pen and ink. Fountain pens were not permitted and the cheap ballpoint pens had not become readily available. The pens we used were a wooden stick with a replaceable nib being inserted into a ring of metal at one end. Each desk had a small white pot inkwell in which one dipped the nib every few seconds. The trick was getting just the right amount of ink on it. Too little and it wouldn't write on the paper whilst too much resulted in blots of ink everywhere. It was a messy process with blotting paper being much in demand. The ink was supplied to the school in powdered form and it was the task of designated senior boys to mix the powder with water to the correct consistency and then to keep the inkwells topped up. My highest role in the school was as an ink monitor.

One other function which fell to the senior boys was handling the free school milk which was provided so that school children could benefit from its nutritional value. The milk came in crates of one third of a pint bottles which were distributed to the pupils usu-

Windermere Endowed Boys School, Bowness.

ally mid-morning following the insertion of a straw through the hole in the cardboard top of the bottle. This whole process wasn't always straight forward. Our school milk was delivered very early in the morning. On a hot summer's morning, standing in the sun meant the milk had already begun to curdle and tasted sickly sweet. In the winter frost, it would be frozen, with the result it often rose up out of the top of the bottle. The only way to melt the frozen milk was to thaw it by placing the crates on top of the radiators. The resulting milk may have been liquid but it was still disgustingly sweet. It turned me off fresh milk for life.

The headmaster, Sydney Hare, ran the school with a firm hand although the use of the strap was much less frequent than in Scotland. He had been born on 4 April 1899 in Kexby in the East Riding of Yorkshire where his father ran a brickworks and held a BSc from the University of Leeds. He lived a long life, dying in Carlisle aged 92 on 1st May 1991. He was very committed to the school, having joined in 1928 and serving until 1962, with a break when he was called-up during the Second World War becoming a Pilot Officer in the RAF. He probably enjoyed this break for in the previous war as a young man he had been commissioned in the Royal Flying Corps (RFC) and its successor, the newly created Royal Air Force. Initially, he enlisted in the Army on 17 August 1917 with the service number 319711 before transferring to the RFC on 16 February the following year. He enthralled us with his stories of his escapades during the First World War. He made it sound so exciting. I could have listened to his reminiscences all day.

In spite of his strictness in the manner the school was run he did understand the conditions in which his pupils lived. We were all working-class with fathers who mainly worked with their hands and usually on the land. One or two worked in one of the many small factories or shops which dotted the villages and townships. Hardly anyone had a car with families relying on buses or the ubiquitous bikes.

One of the external activities organised by the teachers was the nature walk. Straight out of the school gates and a few hundred yards up the hill we were in fields, woods and the open hill sides. Most of us were familiar with what we saw but the teachers made it more interesting by adding nuggets of information. Given our limited level of expectations, in a sense we were easy to please and all enjoyed our escape from the classroom.

The headmaster seemed to recognise our limited and narrow experiences of life and sought to expand our horizons wherever possible. He had a small black car, a Wolseley, and occasionally on a Saturday or Sunday he would take his senior pupils for a ride usually to the seaside on the Furness Peninsula, a dozen or so miles away. These trips were only once or twice a year but the thrill of riding in a car and to the seaside, was a much-appreciated treat. For all of us our normal travel was limited to how far we could go on our bikes. Mr Hare might have been strict and had a temper at times but he did seem to understand the lives of the boys in his charge. Seventy years on, I think of him as a kind man. That one of his nick names was 'Pop' Hare suggests my memories to have been accurate.

The one activity at school on which we had mixed views was learning to swim. Living alongside the largest lake in England, it was deemed essential that we should learn to swim at school. There were no swimming pools in the area and naturally we had to learn in the lake. Every Monday after returning from our Easter holiday we were marched the mile or so to Millerground where there were some extremely primitive facilities. There were two piers about 25 yards apart with the water between them being our swimming pool. It was simply the lake. The teacher had us wading out to our midriffs and then, standing five yards or so from one of the piers we had to swim to it. The distances gradually increased as our swimming prowess improved. It was unpleasant but effective. Most us learned to swim there, which we then frequently put to good use in our own spare time. But it was cold. The lake was full of water from the melted snow off the surrounding mountains and in March and April, was close to freezing on many occasions. As we swam we could look up to the Fairfield Horseshoe and see the fells covered in snow.

Broad Leys was three miles from school but I caught a service bus to Bowness shortly after 8.30am. These buses, operated by Ribble Motors or occasionally Grange Motors, were extremely old as no new buses had been built since before the war in the 1930s. The Ribble buses appealed to us as they were a bright red and slightly more modern. Grange Motors service buses were a chocolate colour and were much older, often with the passenger doors at the rear.

The service was also busy as so few people had cars. The child's fare was 2d each way and I could catch a bus after school from outside Atkinson's hairdressers opposite the church shortly after 4pm. I would be back at home ten minutes later where, without fail, my faithful dog Pat would be sitting waiting for me on the other side of the road in front of our house. She had quickly worked out the time I returned. According to Dad, with whom she spent most of the day, no matter where she was, as 4pm approached she would disappear and slip off to wait for my bus. It's amazing how some animals have a way of knowing the time.

The school was the main opportunity to widen my network of friends. Prior to school my 'mates' were limited to those who lived nearby. These wider contacts were critical as also was the bike. We all had bikes upon which we depended for our liberty. As our legs became stronger and our peddle-power increased so did our freedom and horizons. Bikes were crucial to all the boys but especially so for those of us who lived outside the village. They were rarely new and usually built by the boys themselves with possibly some initial help from your dad. We became extremely capable bike engineers and spent hours in the cycle workshop of Haslam Kellet in Green Bank, Bowness.

If we needed to travel into the village, there was a completely informal arrangement that the bikes of all locals could be left in the buildings immediately behind Ernie Fallowfield's butcher's shop opposite Brantfell Road. This facility held many bikes as it had originally been the butcher's slaughter house and we were all conscious of the generosity of Ernie Fallowfield (senior). Through using the facility, my mother and father became close friends of the family and I, in turn became very friendly with young Ernie and, and to a lesser extent his sister Marie, who were slightly younger. Ernie over time became one of my close friends and we spent many hours exploring the countryside on the Storrs Estate.

Our bikes were more than a means of getting to school or church as, over time, they provided our recreation. Bike rides were a large part of our leisure activity. We thought nothing of going off for a day's ride covering much of the Lake District with all its hilly terrain. Not surprisingly an alternative trip to the seaside around Morecambe Bay which did not involve as many hills, became increasingly popular. In time, bikes gave us our holidays. By staying in Youth Hostels we came to explore much of northern England and southern Scotland. As we grew older many a weekend, especially with a bank holiday Monday, allowed us to explore further afield to Wales or even central Scotland.

Those years growing up in South Lakeland were ones of freedom. We roamed far and wide in the area of woods, fellsides, known locally as 'lots', and small fields enclosed by dry stone walls. These walls were built of stones from the immediate vicinity without any cement or plaster being used. There was a real art in their construction and they withstood many decades of rain and winds. Most of them had in-built stiles which meant movement between fields was easy with us knowing every stile and sheephole through which we could crawl. We seemed to live all our days when not at school in the great outdoors. I remember little rain but I sense that is a false memory. The nearby lakes and tarns depended on the rain.

The farmers and landowners were relaxed about local people and their children going onto their land. It was generally understood we could wander anywhere as long as we left no damage. Naturally, they didn't wish their privacy to be breached and we avoided their gardens. It was also accepted that one should not cross the middle of a hay or corn field but should walk around the field edges and in any case there was little arable land with most of the farming being pastoral. With these provisos, we wandered freely.

Like many of our generation we turned our minds to building dens. This was especially so following a Westmorland-wide junior school trip to Edinburgh. The trip involved catching a chartered train from Windermere Station at five in the morning with a full day

View of village and lake from Bowness Boys School.

in the city. It must have been heavily subsidised for the cost was a matter of a few shillings but even this meant saving over many weeks. We were all thrilled by the Scottish capital and we were especially captivated by the grandeur of its magnificent castle.

On our return we determined to build our own castle, identifying a site on the top of a rocky outcrop in Blackbeck Wood. Our plans for a special den proved far too ambitious as it was impossible to place stones securely on top of each other on the rocky summit. We aborted the scheme and moved our den a hundred or so yards over the wall onto Rosthwaite Lot where a much easier site was found. One side of our new den was a rock face which guaranteed at least one firm wall and there were plenty of stones to construct two further walls which proved to be reasonably firm. A few sheets of disused corrugated iron were discovered to provide a secure roof and sacking was draped across the fourth side for the entrance. This provided a relatively dry and draught free den in which we spent many hours.

Slightly later we found some large-mesh wire netting and made a fence around our headquarters. In those days, we sometimes came across large, heavy and thick penny coins of the young Victoria's reign which, we were told probably wrongly, had no legal value. We ceremonially placed a number of these coins in a tin box and buried them in the environs of our den. It was our buried treasure and I am tempted one day to go and try and retrieve it. The farmer, Jimmy Atkinson, must have been aware of all our efforts but at no time ever challenged us or interfered with our endeavours. The structure lasted until well after I moved from Broad Leys in 1951.

When haymaking came, the local men all rallied around to assist the neighbouring farmers to gather it in before the inevitable rain arrived. Even the larger boys helped with the raking of the hay into rows before their fathers lifted it with long hayforks onto the trailers hitched to rudimentary tractors or even horses. At other times of the year there was also limited opportunities for the men to earn extra income from the harvesting of oats and from picking potatoes. Before the oats were gathered in it had to be as dry as possible so once they had been bound into sheaves and in order to assist the drying, four or five of these were leant against each other to form a 'stook' in the local dialect. The work was predictable and seasonal. I earned my first wages helping with this type of farm work. It was a case of all shoulders to the wheel. In the aftermath of the war, horses were still widely used but a few large Fordson Major tractors had survived from pre-war days but gradually the grey, smaller and lighter Ferguson tractors appeared in the fields. These modern tractors were much easier to handle and I learned to drive on one.

The incomes of small farmers were no higher than those of many employed workers. One such farmer, Jimmy Atkinson, whose two-bedroomed home and adjoining rented land at Rosthwaite was quite a distance from the main road, had some sheep and a few cows. We came to know the farm quite well as his daughter, Margaret, was roughly our age and we occasionally played with her. He had a small milk round and every day would deliver his milk from metal cans hung on each side of the handlebars of his bike. On reaching his customers' homes he would ladle the milk from his cans into the customer's smaller ones. It was extremely hard work to earn a pittance. Later, I was able to do a little to make his milk-delivery easier when working for Tommie Lowden. We resurfaced his access track of about half a mile from the main road with slag from the ironworks at Barrow, providing him with a much smoother ride.

Rosthwaite Farm as it was, is unrecognisable today and illustrates how the Lake District has changed from the years following the Second World War. In the last decades of the twentieth century, Ken and Joyce Scowcroft bought the farmstead and the surrounding farmland. After spending years establishing a successful insurance business 90 miles to the south in Greater Manchester, in 1988 they sold it for £130 million and promptly invested some of it in Rosthwaite. They loved the Lakes and had for many years spent as much time as they could there, in an earlier holiday home. On retirement, they set about rebuilding and modernising the small two-up, two-down house and the attached farm buildings. The whole complex was expanded and extended to include additional bedrooms, a swimming pool and gymnasium. Nowadays it is a far cry from Atkinson's farm of the 1950s. The work has been tastefully completed, providing a beautiful home in an idyllic location and overlooking an attractive pond which was created out of a piece of boggy land. The public footpath however still runs unchallenged past the front door.

This change perhaps epitomises what has happened across the Lake District over the past 70 years. The beauty of the area coupled with the growing affluence of mainstream Britain, has led to a new generation of rich people being attracted to the national park. The retired mill-owners and brewers from industrial Lancashire and Yorkshire who flocked to the vicinity in the nineteenth century following the coming of the railway in 1847 are gradually being replaced by entrepreneurs of the digital age.

In the austerity of the post-war years, none of my friends' families had much money. Work on the land as gardeners, farm workers or even small farmers yielded little reward but we did have an instinctive sense of the need to retain the quality of the environment. The wages of the minority who had a trade working in a garage or bobbin mill were marginally better off but only slightly so. It was very much a community of working people.

Lady luck failed to smile on my mother and father, as in 1948, the year following our arrival at Broad Leys, their employer John Milne died. I wasn't to realise it at the time, but it signalled a great deal of uncertainty for my parents. It wasn't only that my father could lose his job but even more serious was that we were living in a tied house. It went with the job and if that went, so did our home. It was a vicious position in which to find yourself. My parents could only live in hope that the owner's family would carry on but experience showed that rarely happened.

Mrs Minnie Milne did attempt to do so and succeeded for a while but couldn't manage. In 1950, the house was put up for sale. We then had to hope that any new owners would simply carry on.

There was nothing whatsoever my parents could do. They were powerless. Even I, who had never been concerned about such issues, fully understood the implications of the event. At the age of ten, I acquired an intense hatred of the tied cottage system and the utter misery it caused already impoverished and vulnerable people. In retrospect, it was probably my first political feelings. Others were to follow.

To facilitate the sale, Mrs Milne asked us to move across the road to a more modern house she owned. Although we weren't offered any choice, at least my mother was pleased as the house was a much newer, very conventional three-bedroomed semi-detached house which was much lighter and easier to manage. My mother continued to work in the big house. This was almost always the case. The man's job was the gardener or other estate worker, and it was expected that the wife would help out in the big house. Then when it became known my mother was a first-class cook, she was drafted in to cook dinners when the Milnes entertained, which was often. She worked extremely hard during anti-social hours. Thus an 'easier to manage' house was appreciated.

Initially nothing seemed to happen with the sale apart from the growing anguish of our family. Austerity was still dominating the country and even the rich were being cautious with their money. No-one came forward for the Arts and Crafts House with almost 23 acres of land. Then on 18 May 1950, the Windermere Motor Boat Club put in an offer of £15,250. For their money, they acquired a beautiful house, a lodge, three cottages, a boathouse, garages, greenhouses, kitchen gardens, pleasure gardens sweeping down to a long lake frontage and woodland. It was a snip and I bet they got the various boats thrown in!

For a while, it seemed possible that the new owners would still need my father. We had hope. The Windermere Motor Boat Club committee took their time to assess their needs before deciding to sell-off the large walled kitchen gardens with the extensive greenhouses as well as the adjoining Blackbeck Wood, across the main road, which went for house-building. These were local businessmen realising the assets and the Clarks were mere pawns in the game. My father was told they had no need for his services and we would have to leave our house which they planned to sell.

The whole incident made me conscious of the unfairness of society and the control some men, and it was men, had over others.

Bowness Boys School nature walk, 1949.
The author is in the middle of the front row.

My father had to continue with his work in the gardens always in his dark-blue overalls complete with an adjustable bib and many pockets which were put to good use. There was no time off for him to look for another job or house. That was left to my mother. In my mind's eye I can still see the anxiety in her face as she trailed on foot anywhere she thought she might possibly find a house. She was worn out and I remember seeing her in tears. She was a tough woman as indeed all working people were. They had to be tough. But this almost broke my mother. It took something to break the daughter of a Durham pitman who had been invalided out of the Army in the First World War with malaria, having been gassed and losing his sight.

Neighbours and others in the working community rallied round. What was happening to us was not an unusual occurrence. They supplied us with details of every potential house which might become vacant. My mother visited each one, knocking on doors of complete strangers begging for a tenancy. Even a ten or eleven, I realised this was untenable. Her dream was to get a council house. During the war, the factory where the Sunderland Flying Boats had been built was transferred from Kent to the shores of Windermere.

An estate of prefabs was built in Calgarth, a mile or so north of the town to house the workers. After the war, the factory closed and the estate was transferred to Windermere Urban District Council but the demand for housing was so great they rarely became available. My mother visited the council offices almost daily begging for a house. It was all to no avail.

In these post-war years there was a dire shortage of houses for working people. Local councils had no responsibility to re-house homeless individuals or families. To lose your home was a desperate situation. Families had to sometimes accept the most unsuitable accommodation. I know of one homeless family in South Lakeland who had no alternative but to move into a wooden building which the Scouts had been forced to vacate as unfit for their use. There were numerous rumours of single men moving into disused garden buildings or even hen huts. Hence my mother's desperation.

In the end it was my father's reputation as a good and sound gardener that brought us a house. A vacancy happened at Garden Hill, the large house of Henry C Parker and his wife Rachel, who had moved from Lancashire where he had been a successful cotton broker. It was another lakeside mansion on Storrs about a mile nearer Bowness. There was also a house which went with the job. The downside was, that again it was a tied house. I can still recall a discussion between my parents when the phrase 'beggars can't be choosers' was used. It was new to me but I remember thinking it wasn't right that good honest people who had done nothing wrong should feel that they were beggars. Again, I didn't realise it but perhaps my future was being shaped. Unknown to me, at the age of ten I had become politicised.

But there was also a heavy price to pay for that tied house. My dog Pat had to go. My pride and joy couldn't come with us. The owners of the big house had a 'westie' dog and they felt the two dogs wouldn't get on. They never met to see. Quite arbitrarily, the decision was taken and 'my best friend' had to go. I could stand everything else but that broke me. I cried and cried. I did see Pat occasionally for she went to live with my Aunty Ivy in Kendal, ten miles away. Tragically she caught distemper and died. Of course, we had no money for injections or the like, so perhaps it was inevitable. In those days, pet dogs rarely went to the vet and they cost nothing to feed. Pat never had biscuits or dog food. She was fed with leftovers from meals – scant as they were. I didn't check on what else she was fed but I guess offal and waste of rabbits, wood pigeons and any other surplus. The bottom line was she was a healthy dog. I could never bring back my beloved Pat but I knew then that something ought to be done about unfairness and injustice.

In the midst of all this uncertainty and worry, I turned eleven in October 1950. Then in the following February I sat the much feared 11 plus examination. I don't recall being under any pressure to pass and, in any case, my mother and father had enough worries on their shoulders. I didn't do any special 'swatting'. I had always done reasonably well at junior school and usually was near the top in the class exams. I never felt I was the cleverest in the class for there was general consensus amongst my peers that would be another working-class boy, John Beckett. In truth, working people may have had hopes for their children but no great expectations.

Furthermore, whether we passed the 11 plus or not, most of the boys in my year would go to the same local school, Windermere Grammar School. One amusing incident occurred relating to this. David Richardson's father had promised him a new bike if he passed to go to the grammar school. David failed the eleven plus but the letter informing his father of this, opened with the sentence, "your son will be going to Windermere Grammar School this September." His father read no further and bought his son a bike. When he learned of his mistake it was too late as David already had his new bike.

The title Grammar School was a misnomer. It had been a grammar school but was re-designated in 1944, with the *Guinness Book of Records* naming it as one of the first comprehensive schools in England. This had nothing to do with the political complexion of the local education authority but was down simply to numbers. There were insufficient boys in the huge catchment area to implement the new tri-partite system of secondary education of post-war Britain. The school however was streamed into two groups, academic and the others, but there was movement between the two streams which was good and allowed for limited flexibility.

In due course I learned I had passed the 11 plus and would be entering the academic stream. It wasn't a great issue although I was pleased but probably not as much as my mother. As a daughter of a coal miner, she probably shared the view of her own mother who never wanted any of her sons to follow their father down the pit.

My grandmother knew the horrors and dangers and wanted better for her children. Not one of her three sons became miners. In a similar vein, I guess my own mother wanted better for me and, especially so following her awful recent experiences of being on the point of eviction and homelessness. I suppose at the time I never fully appreciated how important that passing the exam might be in the future.

3
Growing up

Apart from having my lovely dog Pat taken away from me which was horrible, the move to Garden Hill Cottage did have advantages. It was a mile nearer the village which was important as the new secondary school where I began in September 1951, was a mile further away in Windermere. The owners turned out to be kind enough although the work for both my mother and father was heavier. As was usually understood in this type of work the gardener's wife would be expected to work in the big house. Normally this would be cleaning in the house a couple of times a week and sometimes more but, in contrast with Broad Leys, there was little or no additional cleaning help. Demands on my mother increased when it was again discovered what a good cook she was.

The Parkers entertained a great deal which in turn entailed much additional cooking for my mother. In 1939 there had been a full-time cook, in addition to a parlour maid plus two unpaid non-family members undertaking domestic duties. I can still recall Mam making the very short walk from the big house kitchen to our cottage. She was more often than not, completely drained. She had extensive experience of working in big houses in Windermere including her first job there in 1925 when she was employed at Brierley Close for the princely sum of £20 a year. This was a few years after she had left home at South Hylton in County Durham at the age of thirteen to work as a housemaid at Castle Howard in Yorkshire before moving to the Lakes where again she had to work very long hours. When she left for that first job at the age of thirteen, her father took her to the station and put her on the train to Durham where she had to change for a train to York which involved a further change. This long train journey was the first she had ever made on her own.

My father had only a part-time assistant to help him run the large garden with a long lake frontage. There was a kitchen garden providing fresh food for the big house but nothing as extensive as Broad Leys and with no greenhouses. The gardens were almost entirely for pleasure as the Parkers enjoyed the beauty of their situation. It was always a struggle for my father to keep the grounds in the expected pristine condition. Garden Hill had been built in the early twentieth century and was very much in the style of those years. It was one of the many expensive houses built in such fashion on Storrs Park. It catered mainly for retiring industrialists from Lancashire and Yorkshire. The most appropriate description was perhaps that of 'a superior gentleman's residence'. That says it all. It was an attractive house with the nearby cottage where we lived, being fifty yards distant. The cottage was of the same design but of course was miniscule in comparison. Attractive as it was, it did not have the same architectural stature of the Voysey house of Broad Leys. Garden Hill had been originally named, Elton, and belonged to a widow, Ada Mucklow who had previously lived in Bury, Lancashire. She was living at Elton when her son, Edward Gerald, had been killed whilst flying with the RFC on 23 April 1918.

The cottage was more comfortable than Broad Leys and much easier for my mother to manage. It comprised two rooms downstairs plus a kitchen into which the backdoor opened. The unusual feature of the kitchen was that it contained the bath. This had a removeable wooden top which permitted it to double up as a table. It was not the most comfortable room in which to have a bath! At Garden Hill at least the bath was of a full size with the hot and cold water supplied through proper taps. The hot water being heated from the fire in the living room next door. However, I had only to stretch out my arm and I could touch the back door. We were not to have a house with a bathroom until my Mam and Dad moved to Hest Bank in 1960.

In contrast to our other country homes, bathing was much more convenient if unconventional. In the other houses it was simply a tin bath in front of the living room fire. The water was always scarce as it had to be carried through in buckets and thus was refilled sparingly. When I was young, I had a small oval bath and generally it was fine, as at that age one had few inhibitions. As I outgrew that bath and gravitated to the larger traditional tin bath, I felt uncomfortable. It was a real palaver but millions of us endured the inconvenience and at times embarrassment.

Upstairs there were two bedrooms and a small toilet with a wash basin which had been converted from a miniscule bedroom. In winter the house was freezing for of course there was no central heating only an open fire in the living room with the three of us huddled around it trying to keep warm. Once at the grammar school, I would do my homework on the table which unfortunately was not as close to the fire as I would have wished for comfort.

Life was extremely hard and frugal for rural working people in those days. It was dominated by long hours with little time for relaxation. My father then worked 48 hours a week over five and a half days and slightly longer in the summer when the light made this possible. He would get up well before 6.30, have his breakfast of porridge or cereals and be at his work by 7am, with my mother getting up at the same time to 'see him off'. I followed soon afterwards. In common with most other gardeners in big houses, he had his main meal of the day, his dinner, at mid-day by which time he had completed five hours hard physical work and not eaten since his breakfast. It was always a cooked meal followed by a pudding. Shortly after finishing work at 5pm, or half an hour later in summer, we would sit down to our tea of bread, butter with home-made jam and cakes also made by my mother from my father's home-grown fruit. We were very self-sufficient. When school was sitting I always had school dinners which I quite enjoyed having a much wider choice than I would ever have had at home, even liking tapioca, semolina and rice pudding which we had often.

There wasn't money for alcoholic drinks and we never had any such drinks in the house. The only exception was at Christmas when a bottle of sweet sherry was bought to offer good cheer to selected visitors over the festive period. In exceptional times there might just be sufficient money to buy a bottle of port which my mother would mix with lemonade. My mother never went into a public bar and drank very little whilst my father only had his regular weekly pint of beer at the Discharged and Demobilised Sailors and Soldiers Club, commonly known as 'The Club', in Bowness on a Saturday evening.

Christmas was always happy at home. Dad had a day off work with it being a bank holiday but not before he had been into work to attend to the boilers in the big house. Whilst my parents would tell me that at Christmas when they were children, they were only given an orange or a banana. I fared better and in any case during the war bananas and oranges weren't available. My mother always had a present for me. Nothing expensive but something I wanted and she had saved up for. After the Second World War, I also had my orange.

The house was decorated but largely with vegetation which had cost nothing. On the front door, there was a welcoming green wreath, complete with red berries, made by Dad. In the living room there was the expected green spruce Christmas tree from the countryside, decorated with red holly berries and a few glass baubles. We then threw pieces of cotton wool onto the branches to represent snow with the tree finally being topped by a star. There were no further decorations except for holly branches resplendent with their red berries, tucked behind pictures or balanced on the curtain rails. All very natural and homely – to me it was Christmas.

My father's first job each day was nothing to do with gardening but concerned the comforts of the Parkers. He would check the boilers and stretch deep inside the fires with long handled tongs to remove the clinkers which if left would have quickly killed the fires. As I got a little older I loved to manipulate these tongs to extract the clinkers. The heat produced was important on the cold winter mornings for such a large house depended on the central heating functioning well and even in the summer was necessary for the hot water. The process was repeated at the end of the day. The warmth given off by the boilers provided some consolation on a bitter freezing morning.

During summertime when the evenings were light, after the 6pm news, we once more returned outside. Although my father would have spent his day labouring away in the extensive gardens of the big house, the summer evenings saw him in his own small garden preparing the ground for vegetables which would eventually end up on our family's dinner plates. I had my own small plot and learned the elements of gardening but at this age lacked the necessary patience to be truly successful. I was always striving to be away to play in the adjoining countryside.

In the dark winter evenings, we stayed in the house settled around the wood fire for which my father had sawn the logs. Life was predictable. We had a second-hand wireless which received the three channels of BBC Home, Light and Third. The first was largely news and associated matters, the second was light music and entertainment whilst the Third programme was essentially classical music and intellectual talks which was rarely on in our house. My father was an assiduous listener of the news especially at 6pm and 9pm. He never missed either and we often teased him at 9 o'clock with the jibe 'why was he listening again as he had heard it all before at 6 o'clock'. In families such as ours in the post-war years, news was definitely for the men.

The electric wireless was in a fine wooden case which by modern standards was huge and powered by several large fragile valves. There were no small sets which had to await transistor technology but my father used considerable ingenuity in making a wire connection to link into another loudspeaker in the adjoining kitchen with the result we could listen to the main wireless there. One of the drawbacks of these wireless sets was that after switching on, it took some time for the valves to warm up and the sound to be heard. If it was switched on at the last moment, it was certain that the beginning of the programme was missed.

There was one wireless programme which was a must for my friends and myself, *Dick Barton – Special Agent*. This thriller serial was broadcast on the Light Programme every weekday evening at 6.45pm. If out, we would make desperate efforts to get back home in order not to miss an episode. The introductory music, the *Devils Gallop*, was one of the most recognised theme tunes on the wavelengths and many of that generation can still hum it to this day. The programme was about a former wartime commando, Captain Richard Barton MC and his assistants, Jock Anderson and Snowy White, who became embroiled in many escapades involving national security. The heroes repeatedly escaped from seemingly impossible situations. They captured the imagination of the Clark family and a whole generation of British people.

The largest single group of listeners were however schoolboys who revelled in the sensational, cliffhanging situations in which Dick and his friends found themselves, always underpinned with nationalistic connotations. The BBC felt that this was not the appropriate message to be sending out daily to young people. On 30 March 1951, it broke my heart, and millions of others, by withdrawing the programme. As it happened however, they replaced it with *The Archers*. Once we had overcome our initial soreness, many of us came to appreciate the alternative which became the world's longest-running radio serial. However, it has never matched up to Dick Barton in my eyes. Dick Barton was a brief but special part of my childhood.

Another programme which appealed to whole families including ours, was Wilfred Pickles hosting, *Have a Go*. He was a proud Yorkshireman and an ardent Northerner, which appealed to our instinctive prejudices. Pickles' popularity however, spread much wider than the north with the programme having twenty-one million listeners and running from 1947 to 1968. He travelled around Britain interviewing local people and attempting to persuade them to tell of their embarrassing experiences on the wireless such as, 'Are yer courting?' These questions seemed risqué at the time but were completely harmless by today's standards. Another endearing feature was his weekly use of the same named assistants including his wife Mabel and the treasurer, Barney. He used catchphrases such, 'Give him the money Barney' and 'What's on the table Mabel?' which soon became regularly used in colloquial English slang.

When I was young, I also listened to *Children's Hour* which was broadcast for an hour at tea time. I enjoyed the nature programmes and especially *Wandering with Nomad* which took over from *Out with Romany*. It ran for a number of years and aimed at interesting children in the countryside. I loved it. I then discovered the books of G Bramwell Evens and enjoyed them immensely. His broadcasts took the form of a walk in the countryside with Romany accompanied by some of his friends and faithful spaniel, Raq. In the course of these walks they came across things of interest such as birds' nests or the sightings of weasels crossing their path. His books were a development of his broadcasts which I later found exciting and then replicated his walks with my friends although strangely we were never as lucky as Romany. Later when I discovered Bramwell Evens had been a Methodist minister for many years in Cumbria, his programmes seemed even more relevant.

One downside of our wireless and its extension was that in the early 1950s I was unable to get Radio Luxembourg on 208 metres. In the days prior to the broadcasting of pop music on the BBC in the 1960s, 'Two - 0 - Eight' filled the gap. In the evenings it broadcast in English and quickly developed a cult audience which peaked in the early 1950s before the pirate stations began bombarding the British Isles with pop music from ships outside the territorial limits. Radio Luxembourg was extremely popular and more often than not listened to surreptitiously under the bedclothes. This required a separate smaller battery radio which we did not own. My father's pride and joy of the big radio with its extension was of no use to me in my bed late in the evening. Thus, this experience passed me by, although I did hear it second hand from school friends.

Outside Garden Hill Cottage – the author with his parents, 1953.

In these pre-TV days, another popular family activity was playing cards. Every household had at least one pack of cards and usually more. There were many complicated adult games requiring skill and judgement such as whist and poker but also others much more straightforward in which the children participated. I well remember playing card games such as Snap, Beggar-my-Neighbour and Rummy. Whenever visitors came for an evening we usually ended with a game of cards. When the family played amongst themselves it was always for matchsticks and even with friends we generally followed the same practice. Even a minimum financial stake of a halfpenny was most unusual. Later card games were marketed specifically for children but there were never any in our house. We played with the regular cards.

Other board games occupied the family during the long-winter evenings involved the throwing of dice. I can recall spending hours playing Ludo or Snakes and Ladders but when we acquired a Monopoly Board it immediately became the most popular. None of my family had ever been to London yet we were repeatedly hooked on a game involving the names of the streets, stations and squares of the capital. It's true to say I learned the geography of Central London from that Monopoly Board, a fact which often comes back to me when I travel the capital's streets. Those winter evenings playing a game were of some lasting use.

At home there was little political discussion. It was unusual in a sense for they were political but seemed to assume that national politics was something above them. Mam and Dad referred to national politicians with deference and respect, always calling them 'Mr' – I don't recall any women being mentioned. They were deeply committed to the democratic process and never missed voting. The refrain was always, 'people died to get the vote'. Given the sensitive nature of Dad's job and his reliance on an individual employers' whim, they kept their political views strictly private.

My father had fallen under the influence of the radical socialist vicar, Rev W B Graham, in his home village. He told me later in life that he had never voted Conservative. My mother's father was a miner and local Labour councillor in South Hylton. She appeared much more talkative and convivial as she accepted lifts to the polls from the Conservatives but gave nothing away. This was the only way to get to the polling stations in the countryside as Labour supporters did not have cars. She admired Mr Attlee, thought Harold

Wilson was marvellous and always encouraged me fully in my political endeavours. But the bottom line in the countryside was that you kept your politics to yourself. To do otherwise could be too dangerous. You just relied on the secrecy of the ballot box. After the 9 o'clock news I would get ready for bed whilst my parents would remain in front of the fire. My mother however would not be long before following me upstairs to bed where she did most of her reading. My father would stay downstairs longer, savouring the last embers of the dying fire, having his final smoke and finishing any newspapers, especially the weekly, *Westmorland Gazette,* which he read several times over. He was a regular pipe smoker but limited his amount of tobacco to two ounces of Digger Flake each week. Like many working men, Dad often shaved at night. Not only did this save time in the morning but was possible as there was plenty of hot water from the backboiler at this time.

A travelling library van called at Storrs and my mother would borrow books from it. These would be supplemented by visits to the library in the village where there was much more choice. It would have to be a good read for my father to bother with a book unless it was on gardening. We had very few books of our own. In those days books were hard-back and too expensive for us as the day of the mass-produced paperbacks was still to come. Our collection was limited to two volumes of the Kilmarnock Edition of Robbie Burns' poems and a few nature books inherited from my paternal grandfather who came from the Penrith area. There was also my father's collection of gardening books and a few other motley books which my parents had been awarded as prizes at school or Sunday schools. I had the odd bird or nature book which I had received as birthday or Christmas presents.

I was encouraged by my mother to read before I went to school and at an early age began to appreciate the wonders of reading. At the end of my first year in Standard 1 of Bowness School, I was awarded 9/10 for reading, accompanied with the comment 'very good'. In later years at the junior school I regularly gained 20/20. I was introduced to Beatrix Potter's books which I found a little too young for my tastes and then graduated to Arthur Ransome some of whose books were set on Windermere which I read and re-read. In his middle life he moved to live at Ludderburn high above the lake. I rowed on the same lake which featured so prominently in his books and explored the islands he described so accurately. I loved the stories and the settings and also the excitement of the characters but was aware that the children came from a different background and period to myself.

There are continuing disputes as to whether Ransome set his lake stories on Coniston or Windermere and both laid claim to be the settings. Not surprisingly I always favoured the view that Windermere was the basis for the island Ramp Holme which was described so accurately as Wild Cat Island in his best-known book, *Swallows and Amazons*. And Ransome had lived above the lake for a few years. Equally, he spent some holidays when a youngster on Coniston. I maintain my contention based on a letter from Ransome which was part of the exhibition at the Lakeland Museum of Life in Kendal. Someone had written to the author asking where his Lakeland books were set and he replied in unequivocal terms that it was Windermere. The letter was removed shortly afterwards. Further support for my contention comes from South Lakeland District Council who maintain on their noticeboards that the town of Rio in Ransome's books is based on Bowness. Furthermore, it also points out that *Esperance*, which is in the Windermere Steamboat Museum, is the iron steamboat on which Ransome modelled Captain Flint's houseboat.

My mother usually read romances and adventure books on the war which sometimes when I was a little older she would pass on to me if she thought them suitable. With my love of reading, I recall being thrilled when she passed on a series of books by Philip Gibbs and Hammond Innes based on the Second World War. The first sports book I remember reading was by Len Shackleton of Sunderland AFC and England, whom I had seen play at Roker Park. It was aptly titled, *Clown Prince of Soccer*, and I was particularly impressed when he called one chapter, 'What the Average Director knows about Football', and then left a completely blank page.

Reading was mainly limited to the winter months as we spent so much of spring and summer on outdoor activities. My father did not share my mother's breadth of reading. He himself had a number of books, almost all related to gardening. In early winter, he received the following season's catalogues of plants and seeds. He spent hours studying these, contemplating what he would plant the following year in the big house gardens and then placing the orders. He always made the decisions in good time so he got first choice of the best plants. Living in the country, there was no delivery of news-papers and thus we never took a daily paper although I sense he would have loved to have done so. If he got his hands on a news-paper however, he would read it cover-to-cover.

Dad was a typical countryman and, although enjoying human company especially those he knew well, he was just as happy with animals, plants and nature generally. He wasn't a great conversa-tionalist in spite of holding strong views. He had learned when working for individual employers he had to bite his tongue on so many occasions. When relatively young, I once challenged him on being so quiet and he silenced me with a doggerel:

There was an old owl who lived in the oak.
The more he heard the less he spoke.
The less he spoke the more he heard,
Now wasn't he a wise old bird.

I had been brash to ask the question. I was left with nothing to say.

He just accepted the inevitability of the seasons and with what they brought, enjoying each as it came. He always believed that whatever the weather threw at us, nature would eventually even things up. The weather was critical to his life and work as was the daylight but he had a quiet philosophical view of living, perhaps that was how he coped with everything which was thrown at him.

The time on his own when everyone else had gone to bed, he also shared with another love of his life, cage birds. His own father, like many countrymen, kept linnets which were trapped before they fledged. They made wonderful melodious music but the practice seemed so cruel even to my father's generation and interest switched to keeping canaries. This was especially strong in mining communities where the birds had been taken down the pits to detect gas and even in Bowness there were still shopkeepers selling ca-naries. Dad had, at different times, two of these strikingly yellow birds with their beautiful voices which he named Dicks and Goldie which I had bought him as a Christmas present from an old miner in West Yorkshire.

These birds were kept in a cage where he carefully fed them with seed which he supplemented by pushing titbits of food through the wires, their favourites being slivers of apple. Before he himself went to bed he would secure the doors and windows and let his birds out of their cage, allowing them to spread their wings by flying around the room. Then after the birds had sat perched on his large hands for a while he would gently lift them into their cage which he would carefully cover with a cloth to ensure it was free of draughts and that there was some subdued light. Later following his first canary's death, I believe to please me and partly to compensate for the loss of my dog Pat, we acquired a budgerigar. He was much more colourful than a canary but had no singing ability. However, as with parrots, they could be taught to talk. I tried unsuccessfully to teach him to say a few words but my father had the patience and achieved some success although it was clear he always preferred a canary.

The 1940s and early 1950s saw the cinema at its peak and we all enjoyed a visit to the pictures. We had a problem however. There was a choice of two venues, the Royalty Theatre at Bowness and the Picture House at Windermere, both of which posed the same problem, namely that the last bus left for home at 10pm and the main picture did not finish until 10.15. To deal with this we had to travel to the pictures at 6pm see the end of the first-house show and then remain in the auditorium and watch the second-house but leaving well before the end, to catch the last bus home. It was amazing how skilled we became at watching the end of a film before seeing the beginning and, not only making sense of it, but also enjoying the experience. As my mother would say, 'needs must'.

In these days there were no fitted carpets in the homes of working people. In the living and dining rooms we had second hand carpets but they only covered the centre of the room. They were surrounded by the wooden floor boards which were always stained a shade of brown. There were no carpets in the bedroom only linoleum supplemented with an occasional 'clippy' rug which my parents had made during the long winter evenings. These were made with a piece of sacking as the base into which were inserted strips of cloth. The colours were so arranged to form a pattern and looked quite attractive.

Bedrooms were especially cold for they never had any heat in them. Mine faced west where I had a glimpse of the lake. It rarely got much sun which added to the coldness. I only had lino in my bedroom which was so uncomfortable when getting out of bed on a winters' morning. I can still sense that awful feeling of my feet coming into contact with the very cold lino – a feeling I never forget. During winter it became unbearably cold and it wasn't a room in which to linger. I got dressed quickly before speedily retreating downstairs. On the colder nights, the inside of the windows became frozen over with Jack Frost leaving wonderful patterns. They might have been wonderful artistic works but the cold prevented me from fully appreciating them. Our blankets were the inevitable ex-army ones, on the thin side and coloured grey. I recollect having an old eiderdown which had seen better days and on top of this was my father's old military greatcoat. It was no pleasure going to bed on cold winter nights. Occasionally I was allowed one of our two stone hot water bottles. These were effective but had to be in place well before going to bed and they certainly were not for cuddling. Then if you caught them with your toe or other part of your body it was agony. Rubber hot water bottles were available from Boots or the Co-op, but they were too expensive and we waited several years before getting one.

In retrospect, it is hard to comprehend the way in which we lived in those early post-war years. The whole country was living in a period of austerity as the government struggled to repay war-time debts whilst trying to rebuild a destroyed national infrastructure. Furthermore, the world was attempting to develop trading links. It was such a difficult period and the Labour Government under Prime Minister Attlee was trying to create a new society. Following the strains and stresses of war, the British people were not prepared to return to the pre-war days of unemployment and social unfairness. The welfare state and the National Health Service came at a price.

In 1948 when the National Health Service was launched it received a universal welcome including from my own family. I recall my first use of the NHS a year or so after its introduction when I was about ten which followed a visit to the circus. A group of us tried to imitate the clowns by walking along the top rail of an iron fence. I fell and badly cut my knee. It was bleeding profusely, and I was rushed to the doctor who was out on call so his wife, a retired nurse, stitched me up and the wonderful thing was there was nothing to pay. That we did not have to do so meant that we didn't have to think twice about going to the doctor.

A couple of years later I had occasion to need the NHS once again. During the winter months, I suffered continuous bouts of tonsillitis, with the result our GP, Dr McGregor, decided I required surgery. In those days the medical wisdom was that the best way of treating this common problem with young people was to remove the adenoids and tonsils – a practice largely abandoned nowadays.

In spite of the pent-up demand, a place was found for me at the Cumberland Infirmary in Carlisle approximately fifty miles distance which required a journey by train. My mother took me, I was operated on the following day which I recall was followed by very welcome ice-cream. Then after two nights in hospital, she returned and took me back home. I remember that journey clearly and painfully,

Playing 'straight bat', 1953.

with my throat still bleeding as I coughed the blood into a cotton wool pad the nurses had given me when I left the hospital. It seemed remarkable that again it hadn't cost us a penny. I needed the operation and the NHS provided it. All we had to pay was the train fare. In the 1950s, as part of the comprehensive health cover within the NHS, we had dental and medical checks at school. If anything untoward was discovered, we had to go to our own practitioners. Occasionally, I was found to need a tooth filling which meant a visit to our dentist whose premises were just a few doors up from Fallowfield's butchers. I dreaded these visits as the facilities were not exactly at the cutting edge of technology. The key piece of equipment was the drill which in this case was powered by the dentist pressing his foot on a treadle. This was exhausting for the dentist and painful for me. You can imagine that it never quite got up to the necessary speed. I still recall the noise and the vibration as the dentist attempted to drill out my tooth. The process was inefficient and excruciating. It was only later I learned that other dentists had electric drills which allowed the job to be done causing much less pain.

One part of the school medical visit which remains in the minds of all schoolchildren of those days was the 'nit nurse' or 'nitty nora'. The nick names were used the length and breadth of the country. We were all lined up in a row and the nurse came along and inspected our heads for nits which were eggs of, or hatched, lice. I recall she had a two-sided comb, using the side with less prongs for general inspection and the dense side if lice were discovered. Then I believe there was the ignominy of having lice in addition to ongoing treatment. We were fortunate that our hair was cut very short as a matter of course and I was never found to have lice but some in the class were not as fortunate. The ultimate indignity was if your head was swathed with a purple liquid which I believe was a general antiseptic called gentian violet. This was liberally applied when someone was found to have ring-worm. It was so obvious and was kept on for a while, a real indignity.

War-time rationing continued right through until 1954. There was also a shortage of so many things and often if one couldn't afford inflated prices one had simply to do without. I recall it was too expensive to buy toothpaste in a tube so we went for the cheaper option which came in flat tins. Shortages were obviously more common for poorer people except when there was rationing. In those days we never had any toilet paper only old newspapers torn into squares. They were uncomfortable and what bliss it was to use soft proper toilet paper for the first time. Similarly, there was never any scented toilet soap in our home. We always had strong red or green soap which was specifically manufactured for washing clothes. When they became almost washed-away they were added to similarly small pieces of soap in a small wire basket which was then shaken about in the washing-up bowl to provide soapy suds for cleaning the dirty pots.

As the 1950s continued there were signs locally of a developing prosperity. Visitors began again to discover the Lake District and workers from the industrial areas, especially Lancashire, Yorkshire and the North East began to travel to the beauty spots. Few of these visitors had cars of their own but came on coaches, or to use the contemporary vernacular, 'charas'. Others would come by train and the line to Windermere was extremely busy with excursions on the weekends. On bank holidays and summer weekends, Bowness was described by the locals as 'little Blackpool'. It was a gross exaggeration but many more visitors did come to enjoy the beauty of the area. Local shops experienced extra business and sales of tourist related items as well as food and drink soared. For local young people this offered the potential to earn extra cash. In those days the price of a bottle of pop included a refundable deposit and many of these were not redeemed but simply discarded when the tourists left. The following days, we scoured every nook and cranny for any unreturned bottles which we then duly took to the requisite shop and claimed the deposit. It was usually 3d a bottle and a sizeable income for us impecunious locals could be made after a busy weekend.

I already knew from junior school two boys who now lived nearby. Barry Gregg lived in the lodge part-way up Middle Entrance. His father, Jack, was a farm worker of the Scotts who owned The Yews and much of the adjoining land. This branch of the Scott family was immensely wealthy being major shareholders in the Provincial Insurance Company based in nearby Kendal. The 2nd Baronet until his death in 1960 was Sir Samuel Scott who as well as being chairman of the family insurance company diversified into many other business and agricultural activities. Over time he became a generous benefactor in the district and was a large donor to the National Trust in the Lake District, second only to Beatrix Potter. His successor, the 3rd Baronet, Sir Oliver, was an eminent and highly respected cancer scientist as well as continuing the benefactor tradition.

The Scotts farm still retained some working horses and I have happy memories of riding on the backs of the cart-horses as they were returning to their stables from the fields. At those times my fantasies ran wild as I became a knight in the days of yore. Barry and I played together a great deal. We would join up with another schoolfriend, Roy Shorrock, who lived in nearby Meadowcroft Cottages and the three of us roamed the countryside. We were all interested in nature, especially birds. To this day Roy is an expert on birds and continues to spend hours watching and getting pleasure from them. During this phase of bird watching, 'young' Ernie Fallowfield regularly cycled along to Storrs and joined in our escapades.

4
Birds and Animals

We could recognise all the birds in the vicinity and knew their whereabouts. None of us had many books in our homes but the one I had and treasured, was the Observers *Book of Birds*. It became my bible. Not only was it there for reference but I avidly read some of it every night with my cocoa before going to bed. I never tired of reading it and meticulously entered any sightings. What was so exciting about it were the colour plates accompanying almost all the birds' descriptions. By today's standards the reproductions were not brilliant but they were sufficiently clear to provide a good image of the bird. I have the book to this day and still occasionally refer to it.

As youngsters we were fortunately blessed with keen eyesight which was just as well for we had no access to current ornithologists' essential equipment, binoculars. In those days, binoculars were relatively rare for the post-war supply of surplus military ones had not yet reached the open market in sizeable numbers. My father had a pair of early field glasses which were in essence, glorified opera glasses and did not have the magnification of modern binoculars but he was always reluctant to lend them to us. Thus, we watched the animals and birds with the naked eye.

I well recall the excitement when we discovered a dabchick or little grebe nesting on a small local reservoir. This was not a common bird in the district and its chosen nesting place was well off the beaten track. We must have watched almost every development from the moment the mother laid the first egg, through the hatching of the chicks until they finally fledged. We told no-one of their existence. It was our secret and we were so protective of its safe-being.

Another bird which intrigued us was the green woodpecker which was relatively common in the locality in those days but now sadly is much rarer. A colloquial name for the bird was *yaffle*. It was called this because of its call which resembled human laughter. To see the green bird flying in an undulating manner making its laughing call was something to appreciate. Another woodpecker, the great spotted, is seen much more often in the twenty-first century than it was seventy years previously. This bird is dramatically coloured with its black and white feathers being capped with red on the head and a further reddish flash on its lower breast. We rarely saw it in the 1950s. We occasionally saw black grouse on the edge of Rosthwaite Lot. This bird was much rarer than the red grouse and at one time was thought of possibly becoming extinct in England but thankfully this didn't happen. The male bird with its black plumage, a flash of red above the eye, the white throat and lyre-shaped tail, was much more attractive than the brownish female. They had a unique mating session called a *lek* where the males would strut around with their feathers fluffed out and their tails forked like a fan trying to attract a female. I recall getting up early and going with Dad to a field on the edge of Blackbeck Wood and witnessing a *lek* taking place. It was a memorable sight which I shall never forget. The local dialect, now sadly disappearing, was substantially derived from the days when the Vikings occupied Cumbria and much of the North of England. The word *lek* comes from those Viking days and is related to a local dialect word, *laik*, which means play. Hence the male black grouse playing with their females. The same word is used in modern Swedish.

A bird which has increased in Lakeland over recent times is the heron. In the 1950s, it was a rare treat to see this tall grey bird standing motionless in water. Then in a flash its long neck would move like a spear into the water and then it would lift back its head with a fish in its beak; quite a dramatic sighting. Herons nested together in heronries and the nearest to Windermere was on the Dallam Estate near Milnthorpe and on occasions we cycled the fifteen miles to see the huge nests in the tops of tall trees with the young herons prancing about their platforms without falling. Underneath however we would find the remains of the eggshells which had been thrown out of the nests by the parent birds. We then carefully took the unwanted egg remains home as trophies.

A further group of birds which are much more common in the twenty-first century are the birds of prey which now have legal protection. Seventy years ago they were shot by gamekeepers and farmers. Many more are seen nowadays. In particular, the buzzard, a large brown bird was rarely sighted but is now one of the commonest of the predators or raptors. Kestrels and sparrow hawks are also regularly sighted on leisurely strolls. In those days, the persecution of predators, both birds as well as animals, went on without thought or even evidence of what damage it might do. We would still come across the barbaric spring or gin traps, which were made of metal with two serrated jaws which would come together with force if tripped. Any animal caught in these now banned traps would end up with a broken leg and left to perish in pain. These were cruel implements of a cruel age. Snares of wire were widely used to catch animals, notably rabbits, and although appearing slightly less barbaric than the spring traps, were basically quite cruel especially when not checked daily. Today they are still used in a modified form mainly for foxes but opinion is moving against their use.

In our gardens we saw the range of common birds and we had our favourites. There were the small birds such as house sparrows, robins, the hedge sparrow or dunnock, as well as various finches. There was the ubiquitous chaffinch with the male bird resplendent with his bluish-purple head and a breast with a hint of pinkish-red accompanied by his much plainer almost all brown female companion. Then there were other finches, the unmistakable greenfinch and the goldfinch. The bullfinch, with the male's black head and striking red breast, was also reasonably common but it was rare to see a hawfinch. The even smaller blue tit, cole tit and great tit were all present in great numbers. We also regularly saw the even smaller species, the diminutive wren and the smallest of our British birds, the fire- and goldcrests being a mere three and a half inches long. Over the years we found the nests of most of these birds.

We also eagerly awaited the arrival of the summer visitors and vied with each other to be the first to spot these migrants from Africa. The swallows and house martins came in profusion and we then eagerly waited to discover their nests made of mud in barns, stables or under the eaves of buildings. The swifts flew high over the tall buildings of Bowness and, although much rarer we knew where the sand martins had their nests in deep holes in sandy embankments. These were sightings but many of the birds which visited Britain in summer were heard rather than seen. The chiff chaffs and willow warblers were just some of the song birds which added to the cacophony in the countryside but we never heard the melodious nightingales which didn't venture so far north.

Other birds retreated to gentler climes elsewhere in Britain as winter came but in spring returned to their summer haunts. Special amongst these were the skylarks who came back to the uplands in great numbers. To hear their loud shrill singing and then to see them hovering in the sky, is one of the beauties of nature. Fortunately, although slightly reduced in numbers, they are still common in the spring and summer months in Lakeland.

The sound which we awaited more than any other was that of the cuckoo. It was the true sound that spring had arrived. It wasn't only that the great writers and poets from Shakespeare to Wordsworth all make copious reference to the cuckoo, it was our own sign of the coming of spring. In those days, early in May there was always a profusion of cuckoo calls as the females flew from nest to nest. Today the numbers have diminished considerably but each year I can guarantee hearing that same sound near Ghyll Head where I had seventy years previously. The year in the countryside is not complete without the sound of the cuckoo.

Larger birds also figured amongst our interests. We identified the curlew with its plaintiff call and its long, probing curved beak poking into damp spots in the uplands. Today there are reports that upland husbandry has led to many damp areas being drained making it difficult for curlews to feed in their traditional manner. The lapwing, or peewit as we called this bird, was common with its unique cry of 'peewit' as it tumbled about in the air. Both these species nested simply in a hollow in the ground and we frequently came across their nests with their similarly shaped eggs as they shared our playground.

Living by the lake, meant we were also familiar with water birds. The waterhen or moorhen with its red blob at the base of its beak were especially common as were the rather aggressive coots which were larger but had a white blob on its beak. In winter black and white tufted ducks came in their thousands as did many other types of ducks including the distinctive goldeneye and eider. There were some wild geese but nothing like the numbers seventy years later. I guess in the past the geese and duck numbers were kept down by shooting.

One species which was much rarer in the 1950s, was the pheasant. With the changing type of landowner there has been an increase in pheasant shoots for which the birds have been specifically bred. There is considerable interest in these shoots which appear to be lucrative businesses attracting many paying customers. In the weeks leading up to the shoots in October there are a plethora of pheasants. Less common is partridge shooting although it is growing and with it an increase in the sightings of the red-legged partridge.

An indication of the close link between my life and nature came in a short article I wrote for the Grammar School publication, *The Lake*, which was my first ever published piece of writing when I was twelve:

One evening at dusk in the middle of May when I was cycling home, a car swerved in front of me and to my surprise, I saw sitting in the middle of the road, an owlet. It was a fawn colour, probably a tawny owl. The driver of the car got out and I chased the young owl off the road and leaned my cycle against the tree where the owlet was. It stood with its wings outstretched and made clucking noises.

It was my intention to examine it and I stooped to look at it when, as if from nowhere, the parent owl swooped down and hit me on the head. I made a hasty retreat to the other side of the road. The man from the car came and told me not to bother about it. He was walking away when the owl attacked him, knocking his hat off. He also retreated.

Now I was left by myself and my bicycle was leaning against the tree with the owlet next to it. I thought I had better risk it and get home. So I went for my bicycle but the owl swooped, but this time I was wary of it and ducked. By the time it landed I was peddling furiously to get out of its range. I returned home with no further adventures. That one was enough.

The event took place in May 1952 at the junction of the A592 and the road leading down to the ferry. Seventy years on, the three large oak trees still proudly stand beside the road but sadly the owls appear to have gone.

One activity which featured prominently in our nature activities was 'bird-nesting' in the spring. We scoured every hedge, tree, waterway and any other possible sites for nests. Between us, we must have discovered most of the birds' nests in our vicinity. We also collected birds' eggs. It seems a paradox that youngsters who loved nature should do this. But, almost every other young boy living in the countryside did likewise. The practice was widespread as even the world renowned naturalist Sir David Attenborough, conceded on television on 15 December 2018 that in his younger days he too had been an avid egg collector.

The code of conduct was understood and widely followed. Only one egg was to be taken from any nest and the parent birds were not to be disturbed. If it was known that the chick in the egg was at an advanced stage, the egg was never taken. We knew it was pointless for the egg could not be blown and of course each egg had to be blown. Two holes were made with a needle at the top and the bottom of the eggs. Then the liquid in the eggs was gently blown out. There was a skill in this to ensure that the shell remained intact. This practice of egg-collecting was so widespread that there was a process of swapping eggs and also, I believe, an organised commercial market for the buying and selling of them. Most of my contemporaries did not have any spare cash to participate in such activity and rather frowned on it.

Thankfully now the practice of taking eggs is illegal in the UK and I have always been a firm supporter of this ban in Parliament. We now know that there are many pressures leading to the decline of our bird numbers without nests being robbed. One of the proudest accolades I have received in my long political life was to be described 'the first green politician of any party to serve on the frontbench'. Throughout my political career I have argued and voted for the maximum protection for our wildlife and prevention of cruelty to animals. It seems bizarre that such a strong supporter of protection should have stolen birds' eggs but I did. I regret having done so and I can only say, I knew no better and nor did my contemporaries. No attempt at excuses but at least my generation have fought to put matters right.

Although our interest was primarily in birds we were always on the lookout for animals. Deer which are common today were rarer in the 1940s and 1950s. In those days if a deer was sighted it was likely to be shot for the pot as venison was a prize meat. In the lake and the larger tarns, we saw plenty of otters. These animals took many fish and were unpopular with fishermen. We loved seeing them playing in the water and were saddened when their numbers declined. One piece of good news in the twenty-first century is that otters have made a very successful comeback and are seen regularly in our local waterways yet again.

On the other hand, red squirrels were very common and so attractive. We would notice the whereabouts of their dreys which were usually high in the trees rather like a magpie's nest with a roof. We had no interest in the dreys which were therefore left alone even assuming we could have climbed to the tops of the trees. It is extremely disturbing that the reds have virtually disappeared to be replaced by the greys but these days there are still real efforts to retain our red squirrels.

Weasels and stoats were often seen scurrying across a footpath or road but we tended to steer clear of them for we believed they had a nasty bite. One of our favourites was the hedgehog. They were so common and we loved watching them curl up into a ball especially when an inquisitive dog showed any interest. Sadly, their numbers have declined drastically. On the other hand, I cannot recall ever seeing a badger which perhaps wasn't surprising as there are reports that they were driven to extinction in Cumbria in Victorian times. In the twenty-first century, thanks to parliamentary protection including an Act I promoted, they have made a remarkable recovery and are now relatively common. Even the sight of a fox was uncommon for doubtless they would have been shot on sight.

We regularly came across two species of snakes, the grass snake and the viper or adder. The grass snake we knew to be harmless but found them scary and fascinating at the same time. It may not bite but we were fascinated by the sight of its forked tongue flashing in and out of its mouth. The viper, as it was called in Cumbria, was a very different prospect. It was attractively marked with black zigzags up its grey back which ended in a V immediately behind its head. I was afraid of it. Its bite was poisonous and it was even said you could die if bitten. Folklore maintained that if a dog was bitten it would certainly die. We kept our distance but in truth the viper was just as afraid of humans and would quickly slither away if possible.

In the early months of the year, we eagerly awaited the emergence of frog spawn which we placed in a large jam jar until they turned into tadpoles. In time these became small frogs and hopped off. With a net on a cane we caught minnows from the lake and kept them in jam jars too. Nothing happened to them... we became bored and returned them to the lake.

5
Life through the Seasons

We were very much part of our environment and the natural world and were aware which fruits and vegetables in the field could be used as food. Late summer and autumn were busy periods. We knew where the best mushrooms were to be found as well as the juiciest blackberries and slightly later, the hazel nuts and sweet chestnuts, the best of which were kept for the Christmas festivities. We knew the seasons and the precise locations where the plants prospered. Together with our parents we harvested the countryside to augment our food supplies.

I recall our symbiotic relationship with nature. We could make the sounds of animals and birds. We knew how to make whistles from the young shoots of ash and sycamore trees. I can still select the young branch in spring, cut a ring around it, tap the soft bark so it can be removed from the hard wood, then after further cuts, replaced. With gentle blowing the wood comes to life as a whistle – a little more sophisticated than the more usual blade of grass being blown between two thumbs and much less raucous!

Although there was still plenty to do in the winter months, the days were short in the North of England and we spent much more time indoors. Once Christmas was over, and the shortest days of the 21 and 22 December also behind us, we looked for the signs of spring. For in the months of November and December nature had almost hibernated. The seasons were much more important to our lives than they were to urban dwellers with the shortest day being particularly symbolic.

We listened out for the signs of spring and especially for the songs of the robin or the blackbird and the thrushes as they began to mark out their territory or sought a mate. But it was flowers that provided the most welcome signs that the year was slowly awakening. First as early as January, the tips of the snowdrops began pushing their way up through the soil to be followed by the simple white flower. As February progressed, the snowdrops became prolific, they lit up the roadside verges and the farmhouse lawns or orchards. Not only did they look beautiful but were a harbinger of spring.

They were closely followed by the daffodil. We are so fortunate in the Lake District that the flower has survived in the wild. The wild variety is considerably shorter than most of the cultivars. It is much simpler and almost completely yellow, no white or orange. I still hold the view that they are the most beautiful of the daffodils and every spring it is a delight to see them re-appearing in my garden in Windermere which was created from the fellside in the 1920s.

How appropriate that one of Britain's best-known poems is William Wordsworth's *Daffodils*. The opening lines were drummed into me, and millions of others at school, but I still remember them with affection,

> *I wandered lonely as a cloud*
> *That floats on high o'er vales and hills,*
> *When all at once I saw a crowd,*
> *A host of golden daffodils;*
> *Beside the Lake, beneath the trees,*
> *Fluttering and dancing in the breeze.*

To me the poem epitomises the very nature of the English Lake District. It is interesting to know that Wordsworth's sister Dorothy wrote in her *Journal* on 15 April 1802: 'I never saw daffodils so beautiful. They grew among the mossy stones about them; some rested their heads upon these stones as on a pillow for weariness; and the rest tossed and reeled and danced, and seemed as if they verily laughed with the wind that blew upon them over the lake.' William Wordsworth used this image for one of his most famous poems. Our climate has changed somewhat over the past 200 years for nowadays the daffodils are way past their best by that time of year. They would have been in their prime four to six weeks earlier.

In the 1950s, wild daffodils were everywhere. The woods were carpeted with them, the roadside verges saw them take over from the earlier snowdrops whilst many fields were simply covered from wall to wall with these wonderful yellow flowers. Sadly, those days are passed. Many still do survive but not in the numbers of my childhood. Those in the woods have been more successful but their yellow presence has largely disappeared from most of the open fields. It's a pity that something so beautiful has been lost in our spring landscape.

Bluebells followed in late April and May. They have survived better than the daffodils as they tend to flower in deciduous woodland and are not therefore subject to grazing animals. To view bluebells in a beech wood with its pristinely light-green leaves lit by the spring sunshine, is something to behold. It's a sure sign that we are well into spring and that nature is fully awake. Another favourite of mine was the Cambrian or yellow poppy which flourishes in Lakeland and can flower from March to November.

During the war and the following years, in a bid to ensure there was an adequate supply of vitamin C the authorities decided that rose hips could help plug the shortfall. They encouraged schoolchildren and the Women's Institutes to collect them in late summer. For their efforts, the young collectors were paid three pence a pound when they were taken to school. In this initiative, our local knowledge was invaluable in locating the rose hips as well as proving quite lucrative.

As spring evolved, country folk began to look to their outdoor surroundings and their own initiatives for their leisure activities. One of the favourites was hound trailing which was popular with the whole family. This is a sport which is unique to the northern counties of England and the border lands of Scotland and whose origins are found to lie deep in history. The hound dogs are bred for speed and endurance and have a strong sense of smell which allows them to easily follow the aniseed-based trail. The course for an adult dog is ten miles long, up fells and down dales and across extremely tough terrain with a lesser, but still arduous distance of five miles, for the younger dogs.

The course is laid by two men who set-off from the same place in opposite directions and then walk five miles dragging a cloth soaked in an aniseed and paraffin-based solution until they reach the agreed start and finish of the race. Once that is completed, the hounds are set free. At a popular trail there might be 50 or 60 dogs, which pick up the scent and then race off at great speed, jumping walls and leaping becks, until after ten miles, they arrive back at the starting point, usually after about half an hour. To watch them through binoculars as they race across the fellside is a majestic sight. Then at the end of the race, the owners shriek and call the dogs names as they race over the final hundred or so yards, rattling tin containers containing food, encouraging them to make that final spurt. The dogs are extremely well looked after, with regular walks on leads, and are provided with highly nutritious food.

The sport is well organised through two bodies which cover separate areas of Cumbria and the border lands of England and Scotland. The Hound Trailing Association was founded in 1906 and essentially covers Cumbria whereas the Border Hound Trailing Association, founded in 1933, regulates the sport along the national border.

The origin of the sport is surrounded in speculation with different explanations in the two districts. In mainstream Cumbria, the origin of the sport is deemed to have originated during the eighteenth century following a dispute between prominent farmers as to whose hounds were the fastest with a race being organised to resolve the issue. This created much interest, proving to be of considerable excitement and the sport was born.

In the Borders the origins go back much deeper in history. For three or four centuries during the Middle Ages the lands on either side of the border were disputed territory with the law different from that appertaining in either England or Scotland – known as the March Law. This territory was basically quite lawless with pillaging and theft of animals across the border being commonly carried out by the reivers. Part of March Law was the practice of 'hot trod' which meant that if you could identify who had stolen your cattle within six days you had the right to take back your cattle plus more. One consequence of this was that dogs were bred with an excellent sense of smell in addition to having pace and sustainability to lead the 'hot trod'. These dogs were vital in following the trail, apprehending the thieves and recovering the stolen goods. Once the border between the two countries was stabilised, the descendants of the dogs remained and began to be used for hound trailing.

The dogs used in trailing are derived from fell fox hounds but have evolved over the years into a similar but distinct breed. They are sleeker with strong muscles and their bodies could be likened to larger whippets, bred specifically for the sport which requires speed, stamina and scent. When racing their fur is shaved to allow for perspiration and comfort. I was accustomed to seeing these hounds on my travels as they were normally walked on leads along tarmac roads for the hard surfaces were adjudged to tighten up the dogs' muscles in addition to hardening their paws.

The races are carefully organised over the season from April to October, with the winners vying to top the league at the end of the season and being crowned champion. The competition is fierce across the counties with much local interest and in the 1950s, before there was some provision for local betting, it was even rumoured that bookies attended the trails and money changed hands! The ones I attended most regularly were held at Lindeth approximately a couple of miles from Bowness and even nearer to our home. I still have in my mind's eye, the sight of Tommy Hadwin who worked on the farm for many years, walking his dogs along the lanes between the trails and always on leads. In 2019, there remain 40 hound trails across Cumbria with a number just outside the Bowness area such as Ambleside, Ings and Kentmere. Whilst hound trails were always a popular feature in local shows, and remain so.

It was reasonably easy to hold a hound trail with no lasting damage to the countryside. The dogs themselves did practically no harm whilst in those days when so few people had cars, there was no necessity to provide car parking. Virtually everyone arrived at the trail on foot or bike.

Given that Lakeland has the reputation for hunting, so graphically recalled by the semi-folk song, *D'ye Ken John Peel*, it wasn't widespread in South Lakeland. The local farmers kept the fox under control by shooting and tended not to want hunt supporters traipsing across their land following the hounds. In Lakeland the hounds were not generally followed on horseback but on foot on account of the roughness of the terrain. I can't recall ever going to a hunt. It simply wasn't something I or my family or friends did.

Like hound trailing the sport of motor cycle scrambling was popular in the early 1950s but has not survived the test of time. Farmers who had some rough terrain ideally with rocky outcrops, would turn it over for a day's scrambling which attracted scores of people. Once again there was no need for car parks and although the land would look rutted and unsightly for a couple of weeks it soon recovered and reverted to its normal use of grazing sheep.

The sport was well organised with many local motorcyclists trying their hand but there were always a few particularly good riders who normally won the races. I well remember the top two riders in my days of attending scrambles, 'Smokey' Dawson, and Zeke Myers, with my support going to 'Smokey' on account of his dad delivering our groceries. The motor bikes were stripped down to the basics with all but essentials removed and, with no mudguards the riders were covered in mud as well as many spectators. We loved the excitement, drama and the noise of revving motor bikes coupled with the smell of cheap petrol being burned in souped-up engines, I can still recall with affection.

In the autumn we knew the whereabouts of the horse chestnut trees with the best chestnuts for the game of conkers. This was one of the traditional games for schoolboys and we sought ways of making the conkers harder. Various ways were tried such as soaking them in vinegar or even putting them in the oven but of course no signs of the treatment could remain. I never found a foolproof means of doing so. By making the holes and threading the string we faced up to an opponent with a similar conker in an attempt to the split theirs – this longstanding game continues to this day.

Autumn was also the season when most boys in rural areas turned their attention to the unlawful activity of stealing apples. With the large houses on Storrs, most of which had apple trees, there was plenty of opportunity for us to do so. We knew the whereabouts of these trees and when darkness fell in September and October we would surreptitiously creep into gardens to steal the fruit. It was wrong, but we did so.

With winter came snow. In Cumbria snow was much more frequent in the 1950s than it is today. We local lads had waited for this moment with great anticipation and wasted no time in joining together to sledge on the hilly fields which fell away steeply towards the lake. When the moment came, our sledges were ready for the fun. These were homemade of wood with iron strips from beer barrels nailed onto the wooden runners to provide greater speed. When we were younger our fathers had made the sledges but as we grew older we were increasingly making adaptions ourselves to finesse them in an effort to maximise speed and distance. Of course, we did have accidents and spills but thankfully none serious.

Halloween was almost completely ignored by local youngsters around Bowness. But efforts were made to keep alive Guy Fawkes night on 5 November in spite of logistical difficulties. Outside of the village, we didn't live near enough each other for any civic type of fire but we recognised that with fireworks being expensive, it was preferable if we could somehow pool our efforts. Beforehand, we agreed amongst ourselves at whose house we would build the fire and in early October began collecting branches and wood for the fire to be augmented by our father's dry wood nearer the day. We literally prayed for a dry evening and kept our fingers crossed.

The danger of fireworks was drummed into us with our parents usually lighting the fuses. The Catherine wheels were carefully pinned onto a fence or door and we marvelled at the patterns as they spun around for their brief life. Rockets were usually rather feeble and were stuck in a pipe, yet when the fuse was lit we still marvelled as they sped upwards towards the heavens. Any bangers or jumping jacks which we could get our hands on, had usually been set off well before bonfire night. The truth was that our attempts were far from impressive as the few shillings each family could afford only really provided a small and brief show. But we did our best and enjoyed it. Even by pooling our fireworks our efforts may have looked somewhat puny but our mothers usually enhanced the occasion by providing toffee apples and cakes. We were rather unsophisticated and easily pleased.

As autumn progressed there was always a spate of whist drives in the surrounding villages to which Ted Shorrock and Dad would cycle. They turned out to be quite formidable players and rarely returned home without some prize. In the run-up to Christmas they were expected to be successful in bringing home a goose, duck or chicken for the dinner table. As the twentieth century drew on and chicken became increasingly available and cheap, eating chicken was commonplace. In the earlier post war years if you kept chickens you were hesitant about killing one to eat, unless you were certain that it had permanently stopped laying. The exception might be Christmas when chicken could be served but turkey was unthinkable. Goose was a possibility but the wild ones sometimes tasted too fishy so it had to be a farmed bird.

The lake was also a key part of our lives, not only providing us with food but also opportunities for leisure. One big advantage of living at Garden Hill was that the Parkers owned various boats and were happy for my father to use one of the rowing boats. He took up the offer with enthusiasm not only for his fishing but also to teach me the rudiments of boatmanship and the dangers of the lake. I proved a quick learner and he happily trusted me with a boat when the Parkers were absent which in the summer was for quite some time; they were game fishing enthusiasts and in early summer took themselves off to the West Highlands of Scotland for their sport. We enjoyed the freedom of their boats when they were away during the months when the lake was probably at its best. In a good season we sometimes had another bonus of them sending a salmon down by rail for our consumption.

Locally caught fish provided an important part of our diet. In season the lake was teeming with various species. The most common coarse fish was the perch with its conspicuous stripes. It was this species that I mainly caught. They were easy to catch from a pier. We made our own rods out of a bamboo cane with a piece of line and a hook at the end to which we attached worms which had been dug up earlier. They tasted exceedingly good and I became a dab hand not only at catching them but then skinning and gutting them before they were cooked.

My father loved his fishing but he mainly caught game fish: char, salmon or trout. There were many trout in the lake and together with Roy Shorrock's father he spent much of his spare time fishing for these. Not for them a worm on a hook, for the game fish they used flies which they made themselves. Many a winter evening would see them tying various feathers they had carefully collected. The family did not always get the trout for often they would be sold to hotels.

One unusual and special fish in the lake is the char. These are pre-glacial fish related to the salmon which were trapped in Windermere at the end of the Ice-age and are only found in deep cold waters and a handful of lakes. The method of fishing for them was by trawling the lake in a rowing boat with two long poles attached to the sides from which there was a line with seven spinners with hooks. These spinners were made of metal again by the two men and were designed to catch the eye of the char. This trawling was done in the dark. Between July and October, our fathers would spend a whole night rowing up and down the lake. They had local knowledge where to row and usually would catch some char which was regarded as a real delicacy. However our families didn't usually get the fish for they were sold to the local butcher, Ernie Fallowfield (senior), who had a ready market in the local hotels. This was another means of supplementing the family budget.

We were still relatively young but understanding the dangers of the lake came almost second nature to us. We knew the currents, where the rocks were and the landing spots on the islands. The islands provided us with much excitement. There was something special about landing your boat on an island. Living south of the Ferry Nab meant our two favourites were Ramp Holme and across the lake, Ling Holme. We knew both of these islands like the back of our hands. We all became accomplished at rowing and could do so for miles. A few years later when a competition for swimming the eleven miles length of the lake was introduced, it was we local boys who rowed the boats accompanying the swimmers.

Summer weekends would find many of the local girls and boys regularly out on the lake. We never seemed to tire of the lake and its islands and came to know where it was possible to land and the best way to approach a beach. We knew all the secret coves and landing spots. There are eighteen islands on Windermere, many called 'holme' which is the old local name for island, derived from the Norse word *holmr*. I have been on every one of the islands.

One game we played on the lake was skimming stones across its surface with the objective of getting them to bounce across the top of the water. This was an acquired skill which we spent many hours practicing. The first thing was to choose the right type of stone which would be smooth, flattish and roundish. Once having chosen the stone, it would be thrown underhand with some force out onto the lake's surface. The trick was to be bending down when the stone was despatched from your hand in order that it hit the surface with force and then bounced. With luck it would continue to bounce. With practice and skill, it would do so a dozen times or more. There are now world championships held on Windermere when stones are skimmed over 98 metres.

Behind the largest island of Belle Isle were a number of smaller ones which became our particular playground; colourfully named Lilies of the Valley and Thompson Holme but affectionately known as Tommy Holme. On a summer Sunday afternoon, usually two or three boat loads of youngsters would descend on these islands and wile away our time swimming in the shallow waters and messing around in the boats. Our school swimming lessons had not been in vain. Belle Isle itself was privately owned by the traditional landowners of the Furness Fells, the Curwen family, and access was forbidden. We youngsters generally abided by that rule but on occasions the temptation would prove too great and we would surreptitiously trespass and explore parts of the island. We made sure we were never caught. We tended to have the islands to ourselves for there were very few boats or yachts moored on the lake in those days.

In the winter months skating on the frozen sheets of water provided much entertainment. Whereas the lake rarely froze completely, most of the bays regularly did. Whilst the more adventurous and foolish would venture far out onto the ice, most knew it was very dangerous and usually never strayed more than a few yards from the shore. In 1963 it froze over sufficiently to allow safe skating on the lake. Most of the smaller tarns and reservoirs froze over every winter when we would all venture onto the ice. We did not have skating boots but metal skates were readily available second-hand at rummage sales or had been family hand-downs. They were simply strapped onto our normal boots. It was far from ideal but most of the young people were able to skate in a fashion for a few weeks of each year.

Help sometimes came from an unexpected source. Blackwell House, now acknowledged as one of the outstanding Arts and Crafts houses, had been requisitioned during the war as a school for the younger girls from Huyton College on Merseyside. It continued in this role until finally closing in 1976. The headmistress, Miss Murphy, was always keen on trying to encourage integration with the locals. In the winter at the first sign of frost, she would flood the flat car park at the front of the house and when this froze, would teach the girls to skate. She would then let it be known to the local young people that in the evening, they would be welcome to use the facility.

We leapt at the opportunity to skate at Blackwell for we knew Miss Murphy would give us some basic training. We could already manage a clumsy form of skating with our strapped-on skates, but at Blackwell we were provided with an opportunity of greater sophistication. On 6 December 1952, I recorded in my diary, 'learn to skate properly at Miss Murphy's and jump, pick things up and skate backwards'. Through her efforts, we came to appreciate the headmistress's kindness which in turn reflected favourably on the school.

Miss Murphy had a reputation as an exceptional teacher to which many of her former pupils have testified. Her basic premise was that every single individual had potential. During the war years and afterwards, she not only maintained high academic standards but ensured her young charges enjoyed the attributes that the Lake District offered. The school liaised with local farmers who shared their experiences with the youngsters who in turn did what they could to help. Excursions were made onto the fells, boating was arranged on the lake and tales are recounted of the headmistress herself teaching the pupils to swim.

After the school left Lakeland, Blackwell House had several owners and there was a fear that the building itself could be lost. A number of prominent individuals, including His Royal Highness Prince Charles, were persuaded that as an Arts and Crafts building, it was particularly special. The Lakes Arts Trust launched an appeal, raising the necessary finance in February 1997 and ensuring its long-term future. Fortunately, during its years as a school much of the original internal fabric of the building had been covered and protected and it was granted Grade 1 status before being formally opened by Prince Charles in September 2001.

6
Country Living

My father, like most of his contemporaries, could turn his hand to virtually anything. He was an accomplished boot and shoe repairer, buying the leather from Woolworths in Kendal, cutting it to shape before gluing it, hammering in the tacks on his cobblers last before using a purpose-designed knife to trim any excess leather before finally applying black dye to the edge of the sole. The finished article was very professional. I still have his last but truthfully could not do what he did. To him it seemed to come as second nature for he was instinctively good with his hands. There was no money spare to go to a professional cobbler. It was simply a case of 'mother being the necessity of invention'.

In rural areas, wages were generally lower than in the cities and towns. It was accepted by officialdom that wages of agricultural workers were too low to be left to the vagaries of the free market and even before the end of First World War there had been state intervention to provide limited protection. At that time my father as a young apprentice gardener accepted the protection of government to join a trade union. The bargaining position of farm workers has always been very weak with employers holding most of the cards, while the tied-house system meant that the loss of the job led to the loss of one's home.

The post-war Labour Government was very conscious of this problem and in 1948 introduced the Agricultural Wages Act which required a minimum wage to be set in the sector which was reviewed annually. One of my youthful memories was of my father scouring the official notices in our local weekly newspaper, the *Westmorland Gazette*, for any proposed increases in farmworkers' wages. This was ironic because he was not classed as an agriculture worker and he was not covered by the legislation. However, he felt it important to be aware of any improvement of the plight of his fellow rural workers so that he could draw the attention of his own employer of his need for a similar wage increase.

The wages of gardeners in private service were notoriously low. That the workers generally lived in a tied cottage meant that the bargaining power was firmly in favour of the employers. My father's wages, like most of his contemporaries, were so low that he did not pay any income tax. Indeed, he always maintained that he would be happy to do so for it would mean his wages were very much higher. It was unusual to hear someone wishing he was paying income tax but it was based on the hard reality of his low wages.

In addition to his own full-time job he was always on the lookout for part-time gardening jobs and thus his awareness of others' wages could assist in negotiations. Given the number of large houses in the area, there was considerable demand for gardening assistance and he usually had at least one additional part-time job. Similarly, my mother would have several part-time cleaning jobs. That situation was the norm amongst working-class men and women. As I grew older and bigger, I too undertook various basic gardening jobs and made a little additional money.

Like all working people of the day, we never ate out. With the exception of breakfast, meals were taken with the three of us sitting around the table, usually in the kitchen. The midday meal was always called dinner and the early evening one, tea. I would not have recognised the word, lunch. Tea was again sitting around the table and normally would have consisted of bread and jam – no sliced bread in those days – with the jam having been made by Mam, largely from fruit grown by Dad. To this day, I still love my bread and jam. This would be followed by a piece of cake, once more courtesy of my mother.

We were also fortunate in having honey from my father's bees. Like many countrymen he was a dedicated beekeeper always keeping several hives of bees which produced a plentiful supply of honey. He was well-skilled in his handling of the bees maintaining a fine balance between firmness and gentleness with the result he was rarely stung. Of course, he took precautions. I can still see him, a trilby hat on his head from which hung a veil to ensure the bees never got to his face, his sleeves and ankles having elastic bands around them for further protection. In his unprotected hands he would be holding a contraption in which was placed burning cardboard which produced voluminous smoke which came out of a funnel in some profusion to pacify the bees. Attached were bellows which, when squeezed, further increased the flow of smoke.

I especially loved the slightly waxy combs of honey sections where the bees stored the newly produced honey but to my personal disappointment most of the honey was produced in the traditional runny form. Tea times were enhanced by a slice of bread covered with honey. Dad's honey was generally clover-honey but occasionally he would be able to move a hive or two to higher ground when we would have the treat of the different tasting heather-honey.

All meals were made by my mother which were in addition to all the cooking she did for the big house. Our food was simple and wholesome and was ideal for a healthy and growing child. Just occasionally as a treat, in the evening she might bring any leftovers from work. Meals were a fixed part of every day with the exception of Sunday. Then we ate at one o'clock whilst listening to *Family Favourites* on the wireless which was a programme of requested music bringing together our troops stationed in Germany, many of them National Servicemen, with their families back home. It was immensely popular becoming almost a national institution.

Most of the fresh vegetables such as potatoes, one of my favourites, carrots, greens, turnips and beets were provided by my father who by skill and careful planning, provided vegetables of some kind or other all year round. These he supplemented with rabbits, pigeons, the occasional pheasant and fish from the lakes and rivers. I never quite understood why my father was so laid-back about wood pigeons getting into his young cabbage patches until I realised that when they were in, he could easily shoot them for our dinner table. He was a first class shot with either a twelve-bore shotgun or a two-two rifle and rarely missed. When these gifts from nature were not available it was cheap meat from the butchers. Before they became popular as a restaurant meal in the early years of the 21st century we ate belly pork and neck of lamb. I never really liked them but of course had to eat them although seventy years later I wouldn't choose either.

With this varied supply of food we were lucky not to be as affected as most British families by the shortages of food during and after the Second World War. I benefited from the nationally devised Welfare Food Schemes. National dried milk was available for very young children as well as other foods. I can recall having orange juice supplied in the flat bottles to ensure I had sufficient Vitamin C and of taking a spoonful of malt each day. I enjoyed both but especially the malt which was sweet and was seen as a source of Vitamin B in building up our bones and our bone mass generally. Then of course there was the provision of free school milk. There was

The author with his mother Janet.

wide recognition of the link between our health and what we ate, perhaps one of the few lessons learnt from the First World War.

These were the days when there were very few electrical aids in the home. Fridges and freezers had not become available for ordinary families with food being stored in the pantry where products had a short shelf-life. We had no gas supply but a second-hand electric cooker. The kettle was usually kept boiling on the open fire when it was lit. There was no vacuum cleaner. Instead we had a Ewbank sweeper augmented by a sweeping brush.

Washing was generally done on Mondays and of course, like most working-class families, we had no washing machine. My mother would heat up a big boiler and with the help of a poss stick wash by hand. The poss stick resembled a small wooden stool with three or four legs attached to a long straight handle. It was used to move the washing around in the hot water which in turn agitated the flow and helped get the dirt out of the clothes. This water was reheated repeatedly for it was used for a number of washes. The most delicate and valuable clothes and fabrics were washed first and the dirtier clothes such as overalls were done last when a bit of dirt in the water didn't matter too much.

Then the washing was put through the mangle before hanging out on the washing line. The mangle was an age-old apparatus which involved turning a handle at the side which then turned two large wooden rollers through which the wet clothes would go and have much of the water squeezed out of them. The mangle was most effective and we were always told not to play with it for fear our fingers would get trapped between the rollers. Countless children ignored the warnings and suffered the consequences but I was lucky with my fingers never getting trapped.

Life was hard for the woman of the house who generally would do most of the domestic chores. As was the case in most working households, there were no electric irons and my mother relied entirely on the traditional flat irons which were heated on the open fire. It was a cumbersome process as the irons quickly lost their heat and to be effective had to be reheated time and time again. It was a much slower and arduous way of working. An electric iron is so much easier and lighter, enabling the task to be completed quicker.

Knitting was still widely practiced with socks, gloves and scarves generally homemade with the prize asset being a fair isle jumper. My mother's prized wedding present had been a hand cranked Singer sewing machine upon which she made many of the family's clothes. Often on a winter evening she would be crouched over the machine on the living room table turning the handle producing a line of beautiful stitching. She had a reputation of being good on the machine and turned up many trousers and skirts for neighbours.

Not only were handed-down clothes altered when necessary but torn ones were skilfully mended and every piece of spare fabric adapted for various uses. At school one of the give-away indications of a poorer pupil was to see them wearing black football, rugby or gym shorts. This was a sure sign that they had been made by a mother from some blackout curtains left-over from the war. During the war every single window in Britain had to have a blackout curtain which meant there were literally millions of them. At the end of the war in an age of austerity and poverty, many families simply continued using their curtains but there remained a plentiful supply of fabric. I always had such shorts as they were still common when I left school in 1956.

My father was a fount of knowledge about nature. He was a true countryman, born, brought-up and spending all his working life in the open air. He had large hands and strong arms as a result of hard physical work and always had a 'good' colour. He was the most patient man I ever came across and would spend hours on an injured wild bird or animal. Training dogs, horses or even his favourite canaries or budgerigars came second nature to him as he seemed to develop an empathy with them. He was a true 'animal and bird whisperer'. In the garden, these skills were transferred in a way to flowers and vegetables. He could get plants to grow in the most inhospitable of places. Where others failed lamentably, he succeeded. He could make two blades of grass grow where others were lucky to get one. Whether it was his years of experience or simple intuition, he truly had green fingers. He knew all the birds, animals and trees and could ream off the names of the garden flowers by their official Latin names as well as most of the wild ones.

On the other hand, my mother was a 'townie' from Sunderland and although loving the countryside, she couldn't compete with Dad. For a period at Garden Hill however she was able to out-do him. The beautiful red squirrels were prevalent in the area in those days. There were no greys or even any threat of them. Everyone loved the cute, smaller reds. They regularly visited our house for food and two in particular made themselves at home. They would venture into the kitchen and over time came to recognise my mother as a friend, eventually becoming so tame, they would take food off her fingers. They would simply sit on her hands and she named them Billy and Ben – although she had no idea of their sex! We all found them adorable. It is so sad that they have been driven from their natural habitat by the larger non-native grey squirrels, introduced from the USA by unthinking humans in the late nineteenth century.

Working men in the countryside would turn their hands to anything to earn extra money. Remembrance Day and Christmas offered opportunities to make and sell wreaths. During the autumn spagnum moss was collected and moulded into circles of wire to which were added sprigs of holly, hawthorn berries and small garden flowers which might be to hand. My father made a number of these each year which were much sought after.

When doing these tasks he would always have his knife by him. Like all countrymen he relied heavily on his knife and always carried one. Even in his 'Sunday best' he would have a small penknife with folding blades in his pocket. He seemed to feel undressed without it and it was regularly used for many unpredictable purposes. It was however in his work that he needed his knife most often and he had several of them. They were larger than his posher Sunday one and all had a handle which was easy to grip – a crucial element of a good knife. The blades were all slightly different as they were used for various functions. A budding knife had a different shaped blade than one for pruning. These differences were subtle but critical to their effectiveness. The one common factor across them all was they had to be razor sharp. Dad spent hours sharpening his, insisting that a sharp knife not only made a clean cut easier but also meant you were less likely to cut yourself as less pressure was needed.

His knife was much in use once the leaves had fallen from the birch trees. He cut the small branches and bound them onto a stave to form a bezom. These were home-made brushes, ideal for sweeping lawns and paths. He much preferred them to conventional brushes.

As youngsters spending so much of our time out of doors, we too were never without our knives. They simply came in useful on so many occasions for we were forever cutting sticks for various purposes. Our favourites were those dating back to the First World War. These were somewhat bulky with raised, ribbed black handles to guarantee a firm grip but with different sized blades and other implements which folded into the handle. One of the implements was a metal spike the size of my little finger which we were led to believe was used by the soldiers to remove stones from the horses' hooves. Whether or not this was the case, we found a multitude of uses for these spikes.

In the scouts, it was more-or-less expected that we would carry a knife although these were a different type to our pocket knives. Scout knives had a non-retractable blade which were carried in a leather sheath hanging from the specially designed scout belts. The blade was about four inches long and would have been deemed illegal under today's legislation but in camp we would have felt only half-dressed in our scout uniforms without a knife on our belt.

7
The Early 1950s

Every year we had a holiday. It was always towards the end of August when the garden of the big house was relatively quiet and could be left for a week. The destinations were far from exotic and always the same. We visited my parents' brothers and sisters in Darlington and Sunderland. Trains were too expensive but there were direct express buses to take us. Wrights ran from Kendal to Darlington whilst the Primrose Coaches of Ryton ran to Newcastle. In those days the coaches were somewhat rudimentary and the roads unimproved with the result that the travel was uncomfortable with a feeling of sickness never far away. Having arrived, there were inevitable visits to other members of the wider family. I especially enjoyed getting to know my cousins who lived in towns and in such a different environment to mine. I always went on holiday in my school blazer. Like my friends it was the only decent jacket we had. Furthermore as it was the start of a new school year, it too was new and smart.

Being towards the end of August meant that the football season was beginning in those days and I had a chance to watch the professional game which I could not do from Windermere. I was taken to Darlington and to Sunderland which was the glamour club with plenty of money and in those days had never been outside the First Division. I saw the famous Len Shackleton and on another occasion in a match against Newcastle, the idol of Tyneside, Jackie Milburn. In Sunderland we stayed with my mother's youngest brother, Isaac, who had been no mean footballer himself in his younger days but his prime claim to fame was that he was the best friend of Allenby Chilton who played 352 matches for Manchester United from 1938 to 1955. He had two caps for England and was a cornerstone at centre half in Matt Busby's early successful side. I was introduced to him once and on my return home lived on the kudos for weeks.

Darlington of Third Division North was different and my visits to their ground of Feethams was a more homely affair. The great attraction was that the match was often against my own favourite team, Carlisle United, either in a friendly or league match. In those days I never dreamt that I would end up a director of Carlisle United for the first two decades of the twenty-first century. My father's brother Fred had joined the railways as a young man and ended up in the railway town of Darlington. As an avid supporter of Darlington Football Club he relished taking me to matches which possibly was the reason he became my favourite uncle.

These visits to football matches were a rare treat for living where we did, made it difficult to get to any professional game although in those days we had three league teams in the county – Barrow, Carlisle and Workington. The latter two were too far to travel to and although Barrow was feasible we rarely went. It was only just over an hour on the bus, however it was not in Cumbria then but Lancashire and thus our support was more luke-warm. However, I was a keen follower of the game and devoured the back pages of the newspapers for football stories. Key matches such as the FA cup final were broadcast live on the wireless and these I never missed.

All my friends had their favourite teams which more often than not were those of our parents. My mother had come from Sunderland with its 'football daft' reputation and had kept herself well-informed about the team although the ditties she sang were somewhat dated. She never tired of singing 'Charlie Buchan, Sunderland's best man' although it was years since he had actually played. Buchan was a legend on Wearside, having played 379 games for Sunderland and winning both the FA Cup and the First Division Championship in the years 1911-1925. That I had actually seen the team at Roker Park ensured my support.

My main support however was for Carlisle United, my father's team. He had travelled by train from his home near Penrith to attend its first game in the Football League in 1928 when they beat Accrington Stanley and had stood on the ash and ex-railway sleeper terraces. I relied on having our holidays in Darlington in the 1950s to see the local team play Carlisle United, the thrill of which kept me going for a further twelve months.

I was also an assiduous supporter of my local amateur team, Bowness Rovers, who played in the Westmorland League at Braithwaite Fold by the Storrs road on the outskirts of the village. My friends and I were there for every home game and kicked the heavy leather ball around behind the goals dreaming we were playing for the blue and whites. Many years later the team folded and the ground is now covered with hard-core and became a large car-park and storage area for expensive yachts. In its hey-day, the crunch match was against the arch rivals, Windermere, when hundreds of spectators would attend with emotions high and intense rivalry on and off the field.

Only one of our group went on to play for Bowness regularly and that was Mel Jeffrey, who was particularly talented and played first at the age of thirteen and thenceforth for many seasons. His ability was recognised by the Westmorland County Football Association for whom he played regularly for over ten years, gaining many county caps. He was the only one of us who took his football seriously. He trained hard. This, with his natural ability, could easily have attracted the attention of the local professional clubs such as Barrow or Carlisle but Mel had let it be known he was not interested in being a full-time footballer. He simply loved playing the game. The rest of us did play football at this level but no-one was as successful as Mel. I played for a couple of seasons in the North Lancashire League for Lansil and the Lancaster and Morecambe Students but I never attained the same standard or had the same commitment or talent as Mel.

Following my eleventh birthday in October 1950, I acquired a new interest. I became eligible to join Baden Powell's Boy Scouts which was to offer me many opportunities and to alter the way I was to lead my life. At the bottom of the hill which I walked up each day to the junior school was an attractive black and white fronted house. This had been turned into a small café run by the scoutmaster, John McDonald Blackburn or DB as he preferred to be called. I never knew his full name until his death on 16 April 1959 at the age of 55. Until then if not called DB, he was always formally referred to as Donald, and that was the case in the *Westmorland Gazette* when it ran a short obituary of him.

The origin of the 6th Windermere Troop was a little unusual. At the beginning of the Second World War, the threat of German bombers led to the evacuation of pupils from the Dame Allen's School on Tyneside to the relative safety of Windermere and they brought with them a firm tradition of scouting. Thus the 6th Windermere was formed at their new temporary school of Windermere Grammar School.

In 1945 when they returned home to Newcastle, DB became the group scoutmaster of the 6th Windermere Troop still based at the school. His commitment to the scouting movement was everything to him, so much so that he had the Boy Scouts badge inscribed on

Scout camp at Great Tower in the spring of 1954.
Roy Shorrock far left and author is fourth from left.

his stone tombstone in Bowness cemetery.

When I joined the scouts, I was in the choir and thus attending church regularly and beginning to be persuaded by the case for Christianity. These experiences sat comfortably alongside those of the Boy Scouts which reflected many similar values in the scout promise:

> *On my honour, I promise that I will do my best,*
> *To do my duty to God and the King,*
> *To help other people,*
> *And to keep the Scout Law.*

The Scout Law continued:-

- A Scout is to be trusted
- A Scout is loyal
- A Scout is friendly and considerate
- A Scout has courage in difficulties
- A Scout belongs to the world-wide family of Scouts
- A Scout makes good use of time and is careful of possessions
- A Scout has self-respect and respect of others.'

These basic tenets of scouting so obviously complemented those of Christianity which is why the two were so important to me at that stage of my life. I was moving from a life in a small family with a restricted group of playmates, running wild in the countryside, to a wider society which included girls. With the religious beliefs now lost, many of those values imbibed in the early 1950s still remain with me. All in all, it was an excellent grounding for later life, building as it did on the underlying values and standards of our parents which ensured we entered adulthood well prepared for the challenges we would face in life.

DB's cafe was one of the oldest buildings in Bowness dating back to the 1600s but it came to prominence in the early years of the twentieth century when Annie Garnett took it over to showcase the work of the small factory she had established in 1891. Annie Garnett was a radical, local woman who was very influenced by John Ruskin from nearby Coniston and the Arts and Crafts movement. When her father died she founded Windermere Industries on the site of her family home, Fairfields, further up the steep hill from DB's house. It was run on revolutionary lines with women using their embroidery skills and the men weaving cloth on hand looms. The firm prospered with the rich new house owners descending upon the shores of Windermere. The products were expensive but of incredibly fine quality and superb design. Annie Garnett took over the old house which DB was later to own, adapted it along Arts and Crafts lines and began using it as a showroom for the beautiful articles which had been made at Windermere Industries. The business prospered until the early years of the First World War.

As a cafe, the Spinnery, was tastefully decorated and very popular with many middle-class female residents who would drink their morning coffee together or take afternoon tea. DB encouraged boys who might be interested in becoming a scout to call into his narrow kitchen simply to chat between his waiting for orders. Although we spent hours in DB's company he was essentially a private person and I knew little about him except that he was from Wallasey on Merseyside and had come to the Lake District in 1933 after a spell in the Merchant Navy. Nevertheless, DB was a great influence on me and my friends becoming a role model to us.

I eagerly joined the scouts who were to provide an added dimension to my life. I enrolled and was allocated to the Curlew patrol. The uniform was passed on to me by a former scout and it was topped literally by one of the broad brimmed felt hats specifically designed by Baden Powell. Within a month I had passed my Tenderfoot exam and read *Scouting for Boys.*

The meetings were held every Wednesday in the main hall of Windermere Grammar School thus I became familiar with the main school buildings before I officially attended in September 1951. I also came to know the other scoutmaster of the troop, Wilf Ellis, who taught geography there. I liked him immediately and later found him an inspiring teacher.

The school hall where Boy Scouts met.

During the dark winter evenings most of our scouting activity took place inside the main hall where we learned how to tie knots, use a compass and read maps in addition to playing physical games such as British bulldog. Our activities however were not restricted entirely to the indoors even in winter. The darkest nights had one advantage, for then the stars shone their brightest. Our scouters helped us to identify the crucial star constellations. My father had already taught me how to pick out the Plough or Pan and from that constellation, the North Star could be easily identified. To know which direction was north was critical to finding one's way about the countryside at night. The scout leaders pointed out another group of stars in the north, Cassiopeia, as it was easily identified as a letter 'W' in the sky from which again the North Star could be easily be picked out.

If the stars in the northern sky were covered by clouds, we were taught to look in the opposite direction. In the winter months Orion would allow us to pick out the south. Orion is a constellation depicting a giant hunter with some very bright stars forming his belt stretched diagonally across his midriff. From his belt, slightly smaller stars represented his dagger pointed to the south. To make Orion more easily recognised, the giant's dog was depicted by one of the brightest stars in the southern sky, Sirius.

Living deep in the countryside with no street lights and thus minimal light pollution meant that I couldn't fail but to be impressed by the sheer beauty and mystery of the stars, especially on a clear frosty night, as well as the different aspect the environment took on in the clear moonlight. I always marvelled at the effect of the full moon on a cloud free night when the light was almost as clear as day yet somehow distinctly different. It was simply magical and at no time more so than when I was cycling home on my own the two or three miles from the village after a scout, or some other, meeting. Cars were rare and thus it was often only myself alone in this rather strange but eerily beautiful world.

Full moons were important in the monthly cycle of the countryside with various weather predictions being based upon them. The two key full moons which occurred around the autumnal equinox on 22 September each year had well-known names, the Harvest and Hunters' Moons. Normally the moon rises fifty minutes later each evening but in the case of these two moons, it is only thirty minutes later. This earlier light is helpful in gathering the harvest or a month later to assist in hunting for food in preparation for winter. In the twenty-first century, the improvements in crop species has meant that usually the crops are harvested these days well before the end of September. Seventy years previously, these same crops were often not ready until the time of the Harvest Moon especially in the north of the country. I can well remember oats being carted back to the farms by the light of the silvery moon.

These moons are followed in February by another supermoon, the Snow Moon. The name speaks for itself. Dad always maintained that the heaviest snowfall in Lakeland usually came in February and March. One of his favourite sayings was, 'as the days get longer, they get colder.' It was an old country saying and my experience is that it is generally correct. But the saving grace is that 'Spring can't be far behind.' Another of his sayings about March was that if it came in like a lamb, it would go out as a lion or vice versa. Over the years I can vouch for its veracity.

Turning to daylight, it was through the scouts, I learned how the sun could also be used to find one's way. The obvious fact, although not widely appreciated, was that the sun was always due south at midday during winter time (Greenwich Mean Time) or at 1pm during the summer (British Summer Time). That was easy and straightforward but we were also taught another trick outside these specific timings. If one pointed the hour hand of a watch at the sun, then halfway between that and midday (GMT) was due south or at 1pm (BST). I never forgot this useful information and it has helped me out on numerous occasions.

As the days lengthened we increasingly were able to move outside. Much of the activity had little to do with direct scouting but involved collecting rummage from house to house for our main fundraising effort, the annual rummage sale. This was widely recognised as the best in the village largely due to the amount of material collected by the scouts with the takings regularly amounting to more than £50 and on occasions £70. The reputation ensured that there were always many queuing in the hope of getting a bargain. Interestingly much of our effort was devoted to acquiring a handcart which could be used for scouting activities such as transporting our camping equipment and of course to collect rummage.

One scouting asset we could make use of was the nearby Tower Wood Scout Camp abutting Ghyll Head which was a large wooded area overlooking the lake about five miles south of Bowness. It was widely used by scouts from the length and breadth of Britain. Within the woods there were open areas where we practiced building bivouacs, erecting tents and making fires. Our scout leaders disappointed the new members by refusing to allow us to stay overnight until Whitsun arguing that from their experience it was too cold before then and given the quality of our army blankets they were certainly correct.

Once Whitsuntide arrived, we went on our first overnight camp at Tower Wood. It was so exciting to sleep out in our ex-army tents. We did not get a great deal of sleep as we talked late into the night when we started getting cold before falling asleep, only to wake up after a few short hours. We were not put off camping, thoroughly enjoying the experience. We also cooked our own food on an open fire. This came easy to me and my pals for we had done this so often in our days wandering in the neighbouring countryside. We would go off for the day in the school holidays with a can of beans or spaghetti, light a fire and cook our meal, always being careful to ensure the fire was out before we left. We could teach our fellow scouts a thing or to about lighting fires. Even in the wettest of days, lighting a fire was no difficulty to us. For example, we knew in such conditions the dry dead white pieces of holly would start any fire. Our days running wild came to good use in the scouts where most of us progressed to be patrol leaders.

One scouting experience which could have gone drastically wrong occurred when we went on a few days camping at Yealand Conyers near Morecambe Bay under our new scout master, Mike Davies- Shiel. He suggested that we should combine patrols and see which group could use their initiative in making the most adventurous journey. My group, which included Mel Jeffrey and Ernie Fallowfield, made our way down to the bay where we found the tide had just gone out. Across the sands was Morecambe and it seemed reasonably, but deceptively, near. We discussed the tide and decided to walk across. We however found the distance was further than it had seemed, that there were rivers which had to be crossed as well as many areas of quick sand. Fortunately, we had sufficient experience in recognising dangers and we not only made the journey to Morecambe but managed the return journey, although admittedly we were conscious that the incoming tide was not too far behind us. It may have been foolhardy but it was the most adventurous.

One very different initiative I enjoyed was Bob a Job Week. This was essentially a fund-raising venture which also raised the visible profile of the Boy Scouts. The idea was for the scouts to perform odd jobs for people who would then contribute a bob, slang for a shilling (five pence), to scouting funds. Doing the small tasks was interesting in itself but I also enjoyed going around the neighbourhood in my smart uniform knocking on doors and asking householders if they had any jobs they wanted doing. We were offered various tasks from gardening, chopping logs and cleaning windows. The original idea was to build links with local communities which it did but in addition it raised money for the scouts. Most of all however, we enjoyed doing the small jobs and feeling useful.

The commitment to the scouts remained with many of us well into the twenty-first century. When the 6th Windermere folded following the closure of Windermere Grammar School, scouting locally rested with the original troop, the 1st Windermere. Much earlier it was recognised that shortage of finance was a possible hindrance for the continuing success of scouting in the area. On 28 April 1950, (before I became a scout) Miles Dobson, chaired a meeting which set up an Old Scouts Group with the objective of raising cash. DB was present at that meeting. Miles Dobson was very active with 1st Windermere and throughout the county. Incidentally he was father of Sue Dobson (Lever), who is a prominent member of the Old Scouts in 2019. In the new century, largely through the enthusiasm of Pat McDougall, fund-raising events continued with annual dinners, bowling evenings and other social activities with thousands of pounds being raised.

In the autumn of 1951 I took a step to getting a part-time job myself and in a way it came through the scouts. I had a yearning to travel and was beginning to cycle around the district getting to know the sights. Then one winter's afternoon I was in DB's kitchen during a quiet spell and he was outlining a proposal for a camping tour of the North of Scotland on our bikes. We would travel the first 300 miles to Inverness by train from Oxenholme which would save a long cycle ride on the main road north. It sounded so exciting and I desperately wanted to go. As the planning progressed a major problem arose when it became apparent the trip would cost £5 which was a large amount of money to me. It would be more than a week's wages for my father and when I mentioned it at home it was clearly out of the question. I began inquiring if I could get a part-time job to raise the money. Approaches to local farmers whether they needed any assistance with milk rounds or farming generally all drew a blank.

Then my mother intervened and went to Grimes, the newsagents in Bowness, to see if they needed another paper boy. Not living in the village required extra time to travel in and initially she wondered if there was a vacancy for Sunday delivery but to no avail. Grimes did offer me a shorter daily round on the southern outskirts of the village as a trial to see how a boy from outside the village would cope. After a few months this was proving satisfactory and the newsagents offered me a bigger round in the centre of the old village around the church. I was paid 7s-6d a week for the short round whilst the longer one paid 12s-6d.

It was a considerable commitment but I stuck it out for almost four years and over those years enjoyed the fruits of my labour being able to buy things I would not have had otherwise. My morning routine was fixed and usually ran like clockwork. I was up before seven o'clock, a quick wash and breakfast then on my bike for the fifteen minute ride to Grimes shop on Crag Brow. It was often cold on my fingers on the frequent frosty winter mornings but I learned to ride my bike all the way to the village with my hands in my pockets, rarely encountering a car.

Once there, I left my bike behind the shop and picked up my heavy off-white canvas bag full of newspapers arranged in order for my round which I did on foot. My first deliveries were mainly to business premises and therefore tended to be the heavier quality papers such as *The Times*, *The Daily Telegraph* and even a few copies of *The Guardian*. There were also several banks and insurance offices which additionally took *The Financial Times*, which was pink and notoriously heavy. Thankfully this meant many of my heaviest individual drops were delivered early, making my bag lighter for the rest of the round.

There was a mixture of all the other newspapers with the *Daily Express* and *Daily Mail* being dominant in the village centre with the odd copy of the *News Chronicle*. Once I had reached the smaller terrace homes below the church in Low Fold and Low Side there was a preponderance of the *Daily Herald* and *Daily Mirror*. I normally read the headlines, sometimes the main stories and always the sports snippets with the result I became quite well-informed on the issues of the day. The round took approximately 45 minutes to complete but occasionally longer when major stories caught my eye. Friday, when *The Westmorland Gazette* was then published, was always difficult as my load almost doubled and the bags were extremely heavy.

With the papers delivered, it was back to the paper shop to pick up my satchel full of schoolbooks and my bike. Then it was a hectic ride up to school in an effort not to be late. It was extremely rare for me to be so even on those days when I was soaked with rain

Ironically the scout trip to Scotland failed to materialise but the impact of having a paper round on my life proved very significant. Of course, there were inconveniences with having to get up an hour earlier even in the school holidays and also regularly getting soaking wet in the Lakeland rain but the compensations were immense. It took the pressure off the stretched family budget, I got an understanding of the nature and discipline of work, I could pay for my bike trips, I bought my own clothes and as I grew older could pay for social activities. It is no exaggeration that it revolutionised my young life at a critical time.

8

The Church and Girls

My mother occasionally went to church but was far from being a regular attender. She simply didn't have time. Sometimes she would attend an afternoon service at the All Saints Mission Church on Storrs, situated between China Cottage and the sawmill, a few hundred yards from where we lived. This was a temporary building specifically designed as a small church under the auspices of St Martin's Church in Bowness. It had a relatively short existence being opened in 1927 and finally demolished in the early 1970s. My father never went to church except for a funeral or wedding and was in no way religious.

About the age of eleven I too became involved in religion – or at least I joined the choir at the same time as Roy Shorrock. How this came about remains a mystery but both his mother and mine were active in the Mothers' Union of St Martin's and we both concluded that the Rector, Howard Rose, was short of choir boys and inquired from them if we would be interested. Almost certainly we

St. Martin's Church, Bowness, with kind permission of Rev. James Richards, Rector of Windermere Parish Church.

were volunteered by our mothers and remained in the choir until our voices broke.

Joining the choir required us to attend church twice on a Sunday with choir practice on a Tuesday and Friday evening. The only compensation was that we got 3d for each service and 2d for a practice. What we really welcomed was a wedding that requested the choir when we were paid 2s/6d.

I would never claim I had a particularly good singing voice but I guess it was adequate for the choir. My other pal already in the choir was Mel Jeffrey who did have a fine voice and became head choirboy. I did however get to know all the principal hymns with their memorable tunes and in doing so came to appreciate the fine quality of church music.

I suppose I was at the stage in my life when unknowingly I became interested in other people's way of living. The rector of St Martin's Church continued in his role for the ten years from 1949 and although from an upper middle-class background, made considerable efforts to keep in touch with all his parishioners. He was a regular visitor to the Boys' School where we were pupils, thus he was acquainted with us. He had served as a soldier during the First World War and seen a great deal of active service on the front line. During his sermons he often referred to those experiences which I found absolutely enthralling. I still recall one of his stories when he was completely lost in no-man's land and he had to make a choice about which track to take. Against his personal instincts, he took the opposite route after hearing God's voice and following it to safety. He told many stories in a similar vein and clearly the dreadful experiences of war had convinced him to dedicate his life to Christianity. At the age I was, he made a big impression on me.

Two or three years later, I with most of my school friends were confirmed on Ascension Sunday, 30 May 1954. I could now take communion thus becoming a full member of the Church of England. The process required us to undertake further instruction into the beliefs and philosophy of the church and I became a committed Christian. By this time, we had come under the influence of a new young curate at the church, Rev Paul Rimmer, who remained there for three years from 1952 and he made a great impression on us. Once I had undergone the formal process of confirmation, I became eligible to join the Church's Youth Fellowship.

It was under his tutelage that the next stage of my religious life

First Communion, May 1954,
the author third from the left on the front row.

developed. He expanded the scope of the Youth Fellowship in the
village. We normally met after evensong on a Sunday and later on
other evenings often at the Rectory which was a wonderful seven-
teenth century house about half a mile from the church and which
still retained many of its original qualities. There we listened to talks
and had debates with others of both sexes on a wide range of topics
as diverse as the Royal Navy and fox-hunting. If I was being honest
it was such discussions which made me increasingly interested in
the Youth Fellowship.

This walk to the Rectory after evensong occasionally led to some
tom-foolery involving shoving and shouting. One of our number,
Derek Hewitson, found himself at the wrong end of such an outburst
finishing head first in a large flat bush at the end of the promenade
with his feet sticking up in the air. It took some time to extricate
him unharmed. There were two other Hewitson brothers, Alan and
Ian, who were members of a well-respected family. Derek followed
the route of many local boys by completing an apprenticeship in
boat building and then working locally. Later he changed direction
and began working for the Ripon Diocese running the holiday

retreat at Barrowby. He completed 28 years working there for the Church of England. On retirement he has continued his commitment to the Christian cause and is currently a church warden. He never faltered from his basic beliefs.

We were at that age when we were becoming more aware of girls and this was the first time we were in an organisation which both enabled and encouraged us to mix with them. This simply was not possible in our single sex secondary school, the choir or the scouts. Although not the prime purpose of the Youth Fellowship, unwittingly it did assist in its success. For the first time in our young lives we came to know and relate to more girls. Through the Youth Fellowship we also had use of the parish rooms on Rayrigg Road where

Bowness Rectory, 1950s.

we would play badminton, table tennis and occasionally organise dances.

It was these dances which led to some of the girls from Kelsick School forming a closer relationship with us. At school, the girls had been given dancing lessons (the boys in their classes were not however) and they shared their knowledge by teaching we boys the basic dance steps. We may not have been ideal pupils but we gained the rudiments of the dance floor which served us well in the future especially when we began going to the Palace Dance Hall in the village. We owe a debt of gratitude to the girls, especially to Sue

Dobson and Christine Nicholson, who were the two most involved in the initiative. I kept in touch with them for almost 70 years.

Once confirmed we attended Communion which was held once a month at 8am on a Sunday. It was rather early and to make this hour more tolerable, breakfast was provided in the parish rooms. This was handled through the Youth Fellowship with small teams of members taking turns each month to cook and serve breakfast. This was very welcome with traditional meals of bacon, sausage and eggs. As time progressed we became more adventurous in our cooking, not always successfully. The bottom line however was that we not only were fed but learned a little about cooking. It served me well for the future.

As the months went by, we increasingly mixed with girls and our activities widened. One of the highlights was going to stay for a few nights at the Carlisle Diocese Centre at St John's in the Vale which we did on several occasions. The centre had originally been an old church school set amongst the remote fells near Keswick. The girls were accommodated in a separate dormitory, but it didn't stop them escaping onto the surrounding hills and meeting we boys under the clear night sky. It was exciting and a new experience.

A little later the leadership of the Youth Fellowship passed to a church lay member Alan Rayner, who was a lively and charismatic individual. He was full of energy, determination and innovation. He was employed by Silcocks Ltd selling feedstuffs to farmers but later moved away from the routine job of visiting farmers on behalf of his employer and continued travelling around farms working for himself, selling plastic sheets with considerable success. Later he founded Lakeland Ltd which markets kitchen and home products worldwide from its headquarters in Windermere.

He finally attained his lifetime ambition after trying successive initiatives, becoming a multi-millionaire in the process. Meanwhile he certainly enlivened the Youth Fellowship. Life was never boring with Alan and we travelled miles to events in the back of his pick-up truck. One memory which remains with me, was a visit he arranged to a christian centre at Lee Abbey, Lynton in Devon. This was an eye-opening occasion where we met young Christians from other parts of England, thoroughly enjoying the experience. Bearing in mind that most of us had not travelled far from our Lakeland homes, to make a journey in a mini coach to the other end of the country was in itself a momentous experience. Even then, Alan

Rayner gave some indication of how he could think outside the box.

The church played a crucial part in the lives of the young people of Bowness as there was no other body which offered anything for young people. There was no other youth club. It really was the church or nothing. The Youth Fellowship played a key role in the lives of many youngsters and helped in widening our interests and understanding of society and all within the context of the Christian faith. Up until this time, growing-up in Bowness had offered us few opportunities to mix with those of the opposite sex.

Of course, we had come across girls as we went about our daily lives and some of our male friends had sisters but by and large we simply ignored them. Now we were thrown together in a more formal context. We might have appeared full of bravado and talk but in truth we were very unsure of ourselves. We didn't find it easy to mix with them. It was all new to us. We were paying the price of having lived in a society largely of boys.

I had come to know Ann Lishman, and Betty Morton, through delivering papers to their homes, Margaret Atkinson, through her father's farm and similarly Joyce Hoggarth, at the Rectory Farm. Julie Evans and Miriam Thornborough, I came to know prior to us all joining the Youth Fellowship as they waited for the bus taking them to school in Ambleside. Then two further girls whom perhaps we were coming to know best were Christine Nicholson who originated from Bowness and her school friend from Windermere, Sue Dobson. Other village girls such as Shirley Stopford, Jennifer Butler, Helen Walker and others joined we boys in the Youth Fellowship.

It wasn't surprising that initially our conversation was somewhat limited for girls did not do the same things as boys. Crucially, they didn't have bikes or go for rides as the boys did nor could they join the Boy Scouts (the nearest girl guide group was at the Carver Church in Windermere) which meant they did not go camping or rambling. We may have lived in the same community but until we joined the Youth Fellowship, we had little in common. Now our lives seemed to be thrown together. They were a kind of absent presence but increasingly our paths crossed.

We attended confirmation classes together, joined in the debates, danced with each other in the Parish Rooms under the watchful eyes of our elders and played games such as badminton. As we approached Christmas, the Youth Fellowship arranged to go around

The choir in 1954, left to right: Back row, Frank Merino, David Lish-man, Colin Rigg and Alan Hewitson. Middle row, Roy Shorrock, David Clark, Derek Hewitson, Mel Jeffrey, Colin Hoggarth. Front row, Michael Martindale, John Bispham, Ernest Fallowfield, Cecil Hicks and Alan Atkinson.

some of the larger houses in the locality such as Lindeth Fell to sing carols. We enjoyed the comradeship, savoured the cold drinks and cakes, as well as hopefully giving pleasure to our hosts.

Then when summer came our activities increasingly were spent outdoors. On one unforgettable occasion, the YS organised a climb up Helvellyn to witness the sun rising over the Pennines. It proved to be a truly remarkable experience.

It was often after evensong that in time we came to know the girls better. In the darker evenings, small groups of boys and girls would set off separately down from the church to the promenade which by then was devoid of tourists. Soon we would pair off and seek the comfort and safety of one of the various shelters which were dotted along the edge of the green further along the prome-nade. But it was very much the case of talking and 'hand holding'. Often our discussions were interrupted by the local policemen who had the boring task of patrolling the promenade a d welcomed the distraction of chatting with the young people. We kn w all the local policemen. The sons of the inspector and the sergeant went to school with us. However, on these occasions we did not readily welcome the sight of a large flashlight being shone into the shelters.

In reality, the girls of our age were more mature and often physically bigger and more fully developed than we were. For example, when I left school at sixteen I was only five feet six inches tall which was about average for our group. I later grew to almost five feet ten inches which was again average for those years. The girls typically attracted boys a little older than ourselves whom they dated and we in turn tended to look towards those a little younger. We can't have been very persuasive suitors for most of the local girls married young men from outside Bowness, and even prior to marriage they too left the village to find work often in the nearby towns of Kendal, Barrow or further afield.

Over time many of the local boys, including myself, were to marry girls from the neighbouring area such as Ambleside, Barrow, Finsthwaite, Grasmere and Kendal. I guess that this was always the way as even a cursory glance at where our own mothers and fathers had come from, with generally at least one of our parents having moved into the area.

In the case of my parents, my father had come from the north of Westmorland twenty or so miles away whilst my mother had come right across the North of England from County Durham. That was the common pattern. Roy's dad was from Preston whilst his mother had come from Barrow. John McDougall's family hailed from Scotland whilst his mother moved across from Shildon in County Durham in search of work and married his father. Even Mel's mother came from industrial Millom on the West Coast and ended up marrying his father from Bowness. Thus, the pattern had not changed greatly.

Overall, we local boys owed a great deal to the church for providing us with the opportunity to meet, mix and gain some understanding of girls. It's difficult to over-estimate the importance of this to those of us who had been educated in an all boy school from seven to sixteen. Single sex education was not the ideal way to prepare us for the modern world. My experience certainly supports the case for co-education.

Many of these girls we came to know passed their 11 plus for unlike the boys, they had no comprehensive school to attend. Those who were successful could opt to go to Kelsick Grammar School in Ambleside or Kendal High School in the opposite direction. Kelsick had the advantage of being mixed sex but with the boys heavily outnumbered. On the other hand, it had a reputation of being a little

Busy Bank Holiday on Bowness Promenade, 1950s.

'stuffy'. The majority of girls from Bowness opted for Kendal High with only Sue Dobson, Julie Evans, Miriam Thornborough and Christine Nicholson choosing Ambleside. That Kendal was so popular with the Bowness girls was simply due to the influence and preferences of teachers at the local girls' junior school.

In one sense the girls and the boys from Bowness shared one common prospect, in that few if any went on to higher education. Although the percentage nationally going to university in those years was only 3.5%, there was a further 2.1% who went onto teacher training colleges, many of them being women. From my male group no-one went on to university from school. Furthermore I can still recall adults expressing the view that higher education wasn't as important for girls as boys for they would only leave to get married. Gender equality ideas had yet to have much impact and local society was not very enlightened in those years. After school, with good local jobs being limited, many of the girls went to work in the nearby towns.

9

Windermere Grammar School

In September 1951 as I was preparing to attend secondary school, the immediate problem facing my parents and other poorer families was the cost of the school uniform as in those days it was only available from selected retailers which were considerably more expensive than the average shop. These were the days before the supermarkets of later years offered uniforms at what would have been seen in 1951 as bargain prices. Earlier in the summer when my mother and father were wrestling with the crisis of trying to find a new job and house, they dreaded a letter from the school outlining what would be required as the school uniform.

The uniform list was long, including a black schoolboy's cap with two green stripes and the school badge, a black blazer again with badge, grey shirts with collar and school tie of green and dark blue stripes, grey short trousers and grey knee length woollen socks. A variety of sports equipment was needed, football boots, gym shoes, rugby shorts and shirts and gym shorts. There was also mention of white cricket shirts and flannels but these were beyond the family purse. Given the wet climate of the Lake District most of us had a blue gaberdine raincoat which also provided warmth on cold days. I remember discussions between Mam and Dad on how they might manage the cost. A salesman from a shop in Kendal called at our house and the money was paid on the 'never-never'. This was the only occasion that my parents resorted to paying by instalments, for like many working families, they firmly believed that the necessary cash should be saved before acquiring the goods. It did highlight the difficulty they had in paying for the uniform.

There were other items which also had to be bought. A fountain pen was essential. The doyen of these were the famous Parker pens especially Model 51 but they were way above the price range of ordinary families. Fortunately, there was a range of cheaper pens and I recall buying pens made by Conway Stewart or Platignum. Then there was the equipment for geometry such as the plastic semi-circular protractors and the compass with the long sharp needle which

In final year at Windermere Grammar School.

we all half dreaded being stabbed with, plus other miscellaneous pieces which needed to be acquired.

In those days boys rarely wore long trousers until they were in their early teens in the fourth form or unless they were exceptionally tall. I enjoyed wearing shorts feeling that they gave me extra freedom especially when playing in the countryside. If footballers, rugby players and tennis players believed that they could move easier when wearing shorts, clearly the same applied to we boys running around enjoying ourselves. Mel and myself were amongst the last in our form to switch to long trousers when we were fourteen and even then, I felt somewhat restricted wearing them, always fearing I would rip the knees.

As youngsters growing up around Windermere in the post war years and not travelling widely out of the area, we spoke with a South Westmorland accent widely interspersed with dialect words. Although still widely used, it was beginning to wane for we did not use it as much as our parents and grandparents. My father's accent, from the north of the county, was much broader than mine and his use of dialect was much more extensive.

We used dialect words widely amongst ourselves and were occasionally reprimanded at school and sometimes at home. The refrain was simply 'to speak properly'. These were the days when having a regional accent was seen as being a disadvantage in getting employment, especially a white-collar job. Such accents were extremely rare on the wireless with only Wilfred Pickles having relatively recently been allowed by the BBC to speak in his native Yorkshire accent and there remained much tut-tutting about that.

In the course of our schooling, the strong links between Cumbria and the Vikings was always emphasised. Years later when studying Swedish at university I was immediately struck by the similarity with our dialect words. In Cumbria, we use the word 'laiking' which means playing. The Swedish word is almost identical and earlier references to black grouse looking for a mate in a 'lek' is similarly derived from the Nordic word to play.

There are a host of similar examples; the words bairn (child), beck (stream), brozen (full), fell (hill or mountain), gang hjem (going home), laal (little), yan (one) and countless others. We also had specific words for trees, the silver birch was birk and the oak was yak; these were still widely used in the 1950s. There is also a method of counting sheep which links the various languages: yan,

Windermere Grammar School in the 1940s,
photograph courtesy of Colin Tyson.

tyan, teddera, meddera and pimp and so on until twenty is reached. Then the shepherd would switch a pebble from one pocket to another and begin counting again. The use of dialect was still widespread in the post war period with particular phrases especially so. Nevva evva av a sin owt like it (I've never ever seen anything like it?), Hoo ista (How are you?), Owzt ga'an (How's it going?), Wha ya de'an (What are you doing?) or Hasta iver deeked a cuddy loup a five bar yat (Have you ever seen a donkey jump a five bar gate?)

There were many more equally useful phrases in use. One we used widely was geldered. This was used if we had done something wrong and would get into serious trouble from our parents. If we were late home we would say, 'I'll get geldered'. This again came from an old Norse word *gelda*. In more modern times, it is used when a horse is castrated and is called a gelding. The implication of its use would be our reprimand would be serious. I suspect this dialect word was only used in communities with strong farming traditions.

Although Windermere Grammar School had been a single-sex comprehensive school since 1945, the headmaster, Stanley Lewis still appeared to yearn for the practices and values of the old grammar school and especially the status that went with it. The deputy-head whose principal subject was Latin and who saw himself as the great disciplinarian, seemed to share the head's views although even to my young eyes they seemed outdated. Outside school, the head strove hard to be part of Windermere 'society' and was a regular attender on the dinner circuit being invited to Parkers where my mother cooked the meals. I remember that she was one of the early cooks in the district to serve warm ice cream. This was essentially ice cream covered in meringue which would be placed in the oven with the ice cream inside and then eaten warm. It was an innovative delicacy which later became very popular being called, baked alaska.

Admittedly the change in the designation and role of the school was a substantial challenge for the headmaster. As a conventional grammar school if a boy had passed an exam he could be awarded a scholarship to attend but if he failed, he could still be admitted if the family were prepared to pay the tuition costs. Colin Tyson freely admitted that he had not passed the entrance examination in 1944 but nevertheless attended the school as his father paid his fees. The payment system ceased on the school becoming fully comprehensive in September 1945.

The transition from a traditional grammar school to this new ground-breaking approach to secondary education clearly did not have the whole-hearted approach of the school's leadership. There were many missed opportunities. A number led by the headmaster S G Lewis and his deputy, R H Robinson, struggled to continue the values of a bygone age. Mr Robinson's nickname was 'killer'. I know of no-one who had been to Windermere Grammar School who did not call him this – of course always behind his back. Mike Bolton in his book, *From Clogs and Wellies to Shiny Shoes*, devotes almost a whole page elaborating on Mr Robinson's teaching methods revealing that,"Killer's favourite teaching aid was a billiard cue, which he referred to as his 'memory tickler'." He then explains how he would single out an unfortunate boy and begin poking him with the cue resulting in the boy normally freezing, whereupon, "Killer, by now his eyes starting to bulge from their sockets '…Can you remember?' he would snarl, the thin edge of the memory tickler starting to hurt as it was being jabbed into the chest."

I and virtually everyone whom I have spoken to about 'Killer' Robinson would confirm the accuracy of Bolton's graphic description. To be fair, he taught me Latin with some effect as I gained a GCE O-level in the subject. I witnessed violent actions on many

Class 3L at Windermere Grammar School, June 1954. The author is sitting fourth from the left, middle row.

occasions although personally rarely being on the receiving end of his violence. Bolton concluded, "I feel strongly that his technique of teaching should not go unmentioned if only as a record of the extreme unhappiness he caused to myself and many others." The teaching was barbaric, unprofessional and more akin to the Victorian age than the 1950s. Everyone in the school, teacher and pupil, knew it was going on, yet the headmaster, who was the only one who could have stopped it, simply turned a blind eye. One can only conclude he either sympathised with the approach or was too weak to take on his deputy.

I am not judging the head as a person for I never knew him in spite of his teaching me mathematics for three years. Indeed, I cannot recall having a single individual conversation with him in my five years at the school except in the final week.

We had a polite arms-length relationship and on reflection, I feel that he simply couldn't relate to north country boys from working families. He never offered me any personal encouragement, although in my term report before my O-levels he wrote kindly. "In his quiet way he works very well and makes good progress." This was followed in my final school report where he complimented me by writing, "A good boy. I am sorry to lose him and I hope he will enjoy his work."

In essence, we came from such different environments. I felt, even as a sixteen-year old, that our values were so far apart. I had a vision of a more modern, equal country in which progressive education was the key. The headmaster struggled with such a concept. However, I have no reason to think that he wasn't a good man but he simply was ill-equipped to handle boys from working families.

My observations were always about his rather reactionary approach to educational change. Perhaps this was because he had not served in the forces during the war and so had not caught the spirit and demand for change which had affected so many servicemen and led them to vote for radical changes in society at the 1945 General Election. There was no evidence he understood that people wanted change and were not prepared to revert to pre-war conditions and values. The school clung on to the grammar school traditions well after it became comprehensive in 1945.

One example of this was the use of the word 'prep' for homework. The wiktionary definition of prep is, 'homework, work set to do outside class time, used widely in public schools and preparatory schools but not state schools'. Whilst the *Cambridge Dictionary* defines it, 'as UK education schoolwork that students, especially students in private schools do at home'. Many grammar schools traditionally tried to mirror private schools by using the word, 'prep'. This was one example which seems singularly inappropriate in this new type of school offering free secondary education to all boys in the locality. It was indicative of the school's culture.

Our school day began with assembly in the large hall in the old school main building. We sat in rows with the headmaster and the staff looking down on us from the stage. We began with a hymn followed by prayers with the head then making his announcements and comments. Very formal and very grammar school almost aping the ethos of a minor private school. To me the formality of the occasion seemed more important than an opportunity to emphasise the homogeneity of the school and to pass on information to all students.

For those of us in the 'academic stream' as it was known, there was an underlying assumption that Latin was probably the most important subject we could learn. Bearing in mind that across England during the Tudor Period and shortly afterwards, a great number of grammar schools were formed not only to teach the 'three Rs' but importantly also Latin as the language of the educated Englishman. Windermere Grammar School was founded in Bowness in 1613 and grammar schools across the centuries maintained the teaching of Latin at their core. Such was Windermere Grammar School in the early 1950s where it was taught by the longest serving teacher, the deputy head, R H Robinson.

Even as a young pupil at the school, I sensed there was division within the school as to how it should handle the equal treatment of all pupils. Later I found many individuals who had attended the school under Mr Lewis shared my views. At the school's Speech Day of 1950 the head was reported in *The Lake* of Christmas of that year, as saying, "The main theme of education was still the teaching of the 'three Rs' and the new methods are merely a more suitable method of teaching them..." These sentiments are not only out of touch with educational sentiments of the inter-war years but much more akin to those of Victorian times. Then, following his untimely death in January 1958 in a very fair obituary in the school's official journal, *The Lake*, I found confirmation of my feelings when it included, 'Mr Lewis would not have thought of himself as a "progressive" in education.' These words would have been penned by a

Headmaster's House, Windermere Grammar School.
Photograph courtesy of Colin Tyson.

teacher at the school and there would have been widespread consultation prior to their publication. On those words and my experience, I rest my case.

Some teachers shared his views but the majority probably did not. Many had fought in the Second World War and understood that the world had changed. A number retained their war-time officer's designations alongside a number who, like so many servicemen in 1945, had enthusiastically voted for Clem Attlee's Labour Government in 1945. They understood Britain had to change its social class system and that education would be in the fore of this fundamental change. In later years at least two teachers, Henry Hiley and Desmond Hartley, confessed to me that they had voted Labour and there were others.

From September 1945 all the boys from the local village schools went to the Windermere Grammar School with the very few exceptions whose parents had opted for them to go to grammar schools at Kelsick, a mere four miles away in Ambleside, or to Heversham south of Kendal. Kelsick was officially co-educational but was largely girls and many of the pupils from working class backgrounds had a difficult time there at the hands of certain teachers. Heversham had a reputation of being somewhat snooty. We, Windermere boys, simply dismissed this as snobbery.

Although all the boys from the surrounding villages entered the same school, once there, they were segregated into two streams, the 'L' for those who had passed the 11 plus and thus deemed more academic and 'N' for the remainder. Today, it might seem a little educationally reactionary with setting being preferred to streaming, but in the late 1940s it was quite avant-garde. Streaming had one real redeeming feature. The boys who had shown ability during the school year could be moved from lower to higher stream and vice versa. This did occur providing some additional flexibility in the system.

Under the 1944 Education Act all pupils after attaining eleven years of age should attend a secondary school. However, that did not always apply in all the junior schools on the periphery of the Windermere Grammar School catchment area. In Grasmere, boys who failed their eleven plus remained at Grasmere Junior School until they were fifteen and could leave school. It might have been that this only happened in the County of Westmorland but it continued until 1959. In the more immediate catchment area of Windermere Grammar School that certainly did not happen. There was secondary education for all as the law required.

The school found itself at the cutting edge of educational change in England. There were major challenges to be faced and a number of teachers, including the head, found it difficult to cope. It was only following the early death of Mr Lewis in 1958, that his successor Mr G G Thomas changed the nature of the school. It must however be appreciated that the challenges were immense and even simple changes were often experimental. For example, when Miles Bolton left Bowness Boys to go to Windermere Grammar School in 1947, the forms were called A for those deemed academic and Alpha (rather ironically) for those who weren't.

For most of us attending the new school for the first time, the biggest impact was its size. Although it was small for a secondary school with a little more than 200 students, to the pupils who had attended junior school where the total attendees had usually numbered from 12 to 40, it seemed huge. What was perhaps daunting was the physical size. Our village schools would probably have only one or two classrooms and now we were confronted with over twelve classrooms plus a woodwork room, gymnasium and sports field complete with pavilion. There were three distinct parts of the school; the original school buildings near the headmaster's schoolhouse, some large wooden huts joined together which were built in the early years of the war to accommodate Dame Allen's School pupils evacuated from Tyneside and a post-war stone block, again joined together, which were the state of the art classrooms.

There was one particular building which was used by many members of school which was simply 'the bike shed'. Many of the pupils arrived by bicycle which were left, or more accurately 'thrown' into the shed near the school entrance. The building had special affection for me, not because it was where I left my bike but where we played football. In front of the building was a tarmaced playground and the entrance of the bike shed provided perfect metal goal posts. Every playtime we played 'footie' with a tennis ball and never tired of doing so. Although in the early twentieth century, the grammar school's official winter game was football, in the years we were there it had been changed to rugby. Possibly there was a message for the authorities that we spent hours honing our skills with the tennis ball – these were the days before the full-size plastic footballs.

My own class at Windermere had only twenty boys and our first form room was Harold Auty's who was the art master. It was in the new block where the light was excellent and as such was a first-class room in which to teach art. Classes changed rooms each period whilst the teachers remained. Later in my school career the chemistry master, C O Morris, and then the English teacher C D Barton, became my form masters.

The school not only taught the more academic students in both arts and science but also a much wider range of subjects to cater for the needs of the local community. There was certainly a practical side to school work from which most in the L stream were excused. There were however, the more usual non-academic subjects such as woodwork and technical drawing which the L stream were also required to take. In addition farming and gardening were offered but only to the N stream.

Furthermore, pigs were kept in the grounds whilst some pupils tended their own school gardens. There was a Young Farmers Club which I assiduously attended as I was quite attracted to a farming career. One of the highlights was the regular visit to the county's agricultural college, Newton Rigg, near Penrith. With this approach to the school curriculum, the new comprehensive school began to build strong contacts with the local community and its labour market in a way a traditional grammar school would have found difficulty.

The provision of these alternative subjects was quite difficult for the more established former grammar school teachers. The school struggled at the forefront of educational practice as one of the first comprehensive schools but the recruitment of Henry Hiley in 1949 with his commitment to the new ideas won the day even gaining support from the headmaster. He had come from a modest background with his family having owned a pie shop at Littleborough in Lancashire. On his own merit he had won a scholarship to Magdalen College, Oxford. After completing two years at university, on the outbreak of the war he joined the Royal Navy, serving first in the Mediterranean and then protecting the North Atlantic Convoys before returning to Oxford to complete his degree.

He was an inspiring teacher, content to pursue his progressive educational philosophy and remaining dedicated to advancing the needs and interests of the non-academic boys. His classes were generally those in the N stream. Initially, the easy part was the introduction of the horticulture courses but then these were expanded to keeping hens and later pigs. The pigs arrived as small piglets and were raised until they were large enough to be sent to market. Thus the boys not only learned the practical aspects of raising pigs but also the vagaries of the markets. The experience proved very positive with any profits being ploughed back into the school and the Young Farmers Club. Henry Hiley's positive approach galvanised support for new educational ideas. He was one of the key players.

Of all the teachers at Windermere Grammar School, the one who had the greatest long-term influence over me, although I didn't know it at the time, was my history teacher, Desmond Hartley. He came from the nearby seaside resort of Morecambe on the North Lancashire Coast and before the war had been working in the ticket office of the LMS railway company.

Following the railways being taken into public ownership at the beginning of the war, there was a shortage of workers in the ticket offices in London so the young Des volunteered to go south. He then offered to work the anti-social hours shifts, often working late nights and early mornings. Although much of the University of London was dispersed out of the capital during the war, a certain amount of teaching remained. Des Hartley ferreted out a history course and used his free time during the day to attend lectures and tutorials. He was awarded a BA(Econ) in economic and social history in July 1944 and joined Windermere Grammar School the following September.

His perspective on history was far removed from the traditional one held in England which was centred upon the study of kings and queens. He believed that it was not on the lives of leaders that historians should concentrate but on those of the ordinary citizens. Later I came to understand that his branch of study was social history beginning with the peasants' revolt, the feudal system, the agrarian reforms through to the industrial revolution and beyond. I appreciated this approach and much enjoyed it, gaining an O-level and subsequently, by night school study, an A-level with a credit.

My approach to history has never deviated from the belief that if one wishes to understand the nature of an age, institution or movement, it is essential to examine the lives of the people not only the leaders. It is basically a bottom-up approach and in my case it all stems from Des Hartley.

Most of the other teachers I liked and got on with. 'Tommy'

Saxton, was always fair and understanding. 'Dick' Barton appreciated my love of reading and encouraged me to act in three school plays whilst the science teachers, 'Curley' Morris, and 'Nellie' Carter, appreciated that I understood the importance of science and I tried hard in their subjects whilst my first form-master Mr Auty was always genial. With the possible exception of the gym teacher, Mr Gibbs, I felt that all the other teachers understood that I worked assiduously in their subjects although not always successfully.

I may have felt even in those days that the school did not serve all its pupils as well as it should have or prepare them for the demands of the modern world. But I was nevertheless very happy and enjoyed my five years there. I made new friends and gained many new experiences. One thing I have always remembered was the school motto, *E Montibus Virtutem* which loosely translated meant, 'We get our Strength from the Hills'. It always seemed to me to be a most appropriate motto for the school set in the Lake District and has forever remained with me. I identified with it from the beginning as to me it reflected a fundamental truth and ever since then I realised that when I face stress or challenges the best way to cope is to retreat to the hills. In my mind, the motto sits comfortably with the opening lines of Psalm 121, 'I will lift up my eyes to the hills, from whence cometh my help.' This was my favourite psalm with which I became familiar as a choirboy.

It was at school, in the corridor alongside the new classrooms, that in February 1952 I first heard the traumatic national news that 'The King has died'. I clearly recall being quite shocked and the repercussions were to dominate so much activity in the country for the following eighteen months. The key change was the replacement of a well-established, middle-aged King George VI, with his vibrant young daughter, the recently married 25 year old Queen Elizabeth. The newspapers were dominated by the theme of the 'New Elizabethan Age' which she would usher in for the British people.

From her accession until her Coronation on 2 June 1953, every town, village and hamlet resonated with royal activities. Bowness was no exception and the dominance of the established church drove forward much of the activity. Foremost was the Mothers' Union which organised a mammoth concert of celebrations in the parish rooms in early 1953. The theme was hugely patriotic with women leading from the stage with renditions of such songs as *There'll Always be an England, Jerusalem, Land of Hope and*

Glory, *Loch Lomond*, *Londonderry Air* and *Cwm Rhondda*. Most of the members' children appeared on the stage in various guises. I was dressed in adapted white pyjamas to represent the Royal Navy and 'Old England' by dancing the hornpipe whilst Roy Shorrock represented Northern Ireland and wore a pair of borrowed riding-breeches which were somewhat too large with the result they kept slipping-down, much to his chagrin.

One unintended consequence of the Coronation in 1953 was the increase in the sales of televisions. They were still rare, very expensive and much beyond the pockets of most working-class families but some did manage to acquire them on the 'never-never'. This method of payment was generally frowned on by rural working-people who felt the correct thing to do was to save up the money first. This is what my family believed and we did not get our first TV until the 1960s.

We were fortunate however in that close friends of my parents, Clyde and Gladys Swift, with whom they had worked in pre-war years at Lindeth Fell, had acquired one. They were lucky in winning a huge raffle which I believe was run by the local football club, and it was just in time for the Coronation. We were invited with I recall over twenty people, including Ernie Fallowfield, crammed into a small, narrow sitting room watching a TV screen probably less than a foot wide in a large wooden case. It was of course black and white in those days. We enjoyed the occasion but couldn't wait to see the full colour version on the large screen at the Royalty in Bowness some time later. As was the case with many other people, the Coronation was the first time I'd watched television.

Following the Coronation there was an inevitable but gradual increase in families acquiring television sets. They were horribly expensive and in the early 1950s most were rented until over time the prices fell and purchasing became popular. It was impossible in those early days to imagine how the widespread acquisition of televisons would revolutionise the social lives of people not only in Britain but across the world.

On a personal level, Coronation Day saw my mother suffering a great deal of personal, private pain when her favourite younger sister, Ivy Pearson, left England for a new life in Australia with her husband Les and her two young children, Christine and John. In the early decades of the twentieth century, on leaving school, the tradition was for young women in the North East of England and other industrial areas to leave their families and homes and travel to take up employment as maidservants and in the kitchens in the big houses of the rich. My mother had done just this when she had been thirteen and Ivy, with my mother's encouragement had followed her example and joined her in the Lake District. Naturally she had been taken under my mother's wing and they were very close.

In 1947 as we were preparing to move back to Cumbria my mother and myself stayed with her for a while in Kendal. In the late 1930s she had married a young ambitious Kendal man, who when the Second World War began, was conscripted into the Royal Navy, spending most of the war in the Far East rising to the rank of chief petty officer. When we moved to Windermere, we were regular visitors to their house as they were to ours. My cousins, Christine and John, became like a sister and brother to me. In Australia, they had a third child, Philip. Later he came and worked in England, living with my parents. In turn they became very close and he was regarded as a son.

My Uncle Les was the ambitious manager of a tobacco and snuff company, Gawith and Hoggarth Ltd, in Kendal when he was tempted by an offer of a new life and employment in Queensland. My aunt initially went along with the plan before getting cold feet when it was too late. Thus on the very day of the Coronation, on 2 June 1953, the family set sail from distant London for even further-off Australia leaving my mother heartbroken. They remained in Australia before moving to New Zealand but on reflection it might have been better if they had stayed in England. My mother certainly felt so until her dying years but in those early days she tried hard to conceal her feelings but even I, at fourteen, saw through her grief.

Several events were organised by volunteers around Coronation Day. There was a sports day when the weather was extremely unpleasant and cold for early June. This was held on the sports field of the Old College Secondary School for Girls in Windermere and I won a sprint race receiving the prize of a hard cricket ball. To be quite honest the weather was too dreadful for the event to be memorable which was a pity for considerable effort had been put in by volunteers to make the big day one never to forget. Another celebration which was spread over several days was a Scouts Coronation Jamboree held at Brathay Hall near Ambleside which I really enjoyed.

That year was a busy one for the scouts. Donald Blackburn, the group scoutmaster wrote in the school magazine, *The Lake*, that the

Bob a Job week, was 'up to standard' while describing the Troop's turnout as 'smart' when we took part in a parade for the interestingly named Empire Youth Sunday Service at St Martin's Church. We also hauled branches and other flammable material to the top of the local beauty spot, Orrest Head, to build a bonfire to celebrate the Queen's Coronation and took great pleasure in helping to light it when it could be seen for miles. To youngsters from a quiet village it was an exciting time. We seemed to be part of a great national celebration

10
Changes Afoot

Once the Coronation had passed, life gradually returned to normal and I continued with the choir, youth fellowship, scouts, the paper round as well as settling in at Windermere Grammar School. But things were beginning to change albeit gradually. My voice broke and my spell as a choir boy was over which I was quite relaxed about as I was tiring of all the services and practice sessions. However, I enthusiastically continued with my other church activities centred on the Youth Fellowship. It is difficult to overplay its importance to my generation of local young people, with so many of their communal activities depending upon it. Although completely run by church people along Christian lines, it was far from being strait-laced and narrow minded. When the affable young Rev Paul Rimmer left as curate and Alan Rayner assumed the role of leader, the activities expanded. Visits were made to new venues including the seaside resort of Morecambe thirty miles away. We all crammed into the open back of his pick-up truck, which would not have been allowed today. A little later he recognised the wider social needs of the Youth Fellowship and obtained premises which had once belonged to the Crown Hotel with the aim of establishing a place where young people could drink coffee and play records. This was advanced thinking for it was a kind of cross between a coffee bar and an embryonic night club but run along Christian lines. Unfortunately, after its early success its popularity gradually faded.

One of the scout leaders, Wilf Ellis, who was also the geography teacher at Windermere Grammar School, gained promotion and moved to another school further south at the end of 1952. I had liked him both as a scout leader and a teacher and was sad to see him leave. He was replaced as geography teacher by Mike Davies-Shiel who seemed not much older than our sixth formers but was also a scouter and he conveniently became one of our scout masters. He was to have a considersable influence on many of us and remained in Windermere until his death in 2009. His interests drifted away from traditional geography and geology to industrial heritage. He became one of the foremost industrial archaeologists in Cumbria and published a number of books. He was an inspiration and whenever we, his former pupils had queries, he always freely gave of his time with a patient explanation and the fullest answer. Many years later following his death, we regularly remark to one another that we wished we had inquired more of Mike for he was a mine of local information.

My activities in the scouts continued with growing enthusiasm. I re-read *Scouting for Boys* which was coming to be my lodestone and I continued to be completely hooked on the ethos and practices of the movement. Over the years I progressed through the hierarchy passing exams and gaining badges in the process which I meticulously sewed onto my uniform. On enrolment I had been appointed a member of the Curlew patrol with green flashes on my shoulder. Growing up in South Lakeland in those wild open spaces which the curlew inhabited with its easily recognised plaintiff call, seemed to make it all the more appropriate to be a member of that patrol. I always retained a secret pride in that.

The 6th Windermere Troop was comprised of four patrols; the Curlews, Eagles, Falcons and Seagulls with intense but friendly competition between them. After a couple of years, I was promoted to patrol leader of the Curlews which entitled me to wear two white stripes on the breast pocket of my scout shirt and assumed the responsibility of leading five or six other scouts. Mel Jeffrey became patrol leader of the Seagulls and Roy Shorrock of the Eagles whilst slightly before us Peter Hoggarth became patrol leader of the Falcons. Roy continued with the scouts following Donald Blackburn's death in the capacity of an assistant scouter.

We continued with the usual scouting activities and looked forward to the summer months when we could spend time outdoors and were able to enjoy our favourite activity of camping. In winter we were always involved in routine fund raising. We constantly felt frustrated that we met in the school hall and yearned for a building of our own. Eventually, in early 1952 the headmaster of Windermere Grammar School agreed that we could have a plot of land by the lane on the northern edge of the school's extensive grounds. This immediately stimulated the troop into action, plans were produced and the fund-raising stepped up. From then on, most of our efforts were concerned with acquiring our own HQ.

We spent hours with pickaxes and spades preparing the land for building to begin. Tons of stones and rocks were moved, including some weighing more than six hundredweight and all by the scouts, their parents and four small wheels. Finally, the day came when we could lay the composite floor for the wooden hut and then very quickly the sides and the roof of the building followed. With the exterior of the building completed we turned our attention to the inside. Thirteen hundred square feet of hardboard lining were cut and fitted by the scouts themselves and a few parents. Michael Hodgson was the star for he worked night after night and handled every piece installed. Most of this work had to be done with the aid of a Tilley lamp as electricity was not then installed. As almost all the labour was done by the scouts the costs were kept down but even then we had to raise in excess of £200. Following the completion of the inside, the great day came in 1953 when the 6th Windermere Scouts had its own fully-functioning HQ.

The scouts felt this should be celebrated with a party, with the scouters agreeing that the organising be left to the scouts themselves. Electricity had still not been installed but we managed to run a wire across the narrow lane from John McDougall's aunt's house. Wisely the scout leaders declined to attend and determined that the scouts themselves should decide on the invitations. Girls were invited and alcohol acquired. Whether Baden Powell would have approved, the party happened, the likes of which those who attended would never forget. No damage was done but the following day all the doors and windows were flung wide open and from then onwards the building reverted to strict scouting activities. After all the months of strenuous effort it was only right we had let our hair down.

Windermere Grammar School built up an enviable reputation for its annual Gilbert and Sullivan productions which in the eyes of many were the high point of the school year and they were certainly excellent presentations with lavish and colourful sets. Members of staff, including the headmaster and his deputy, acted and sang alongside the pupils. The Royalty Theatre was taken over for the week and was always packed. In my school years, *Iolanthe*, *Mikardo*, *Ruddigore*, *Gondoliers* and *Pirates of Penzance* all featured to high acclaim. The operas were directed by the highly regarded music teacher, Reg Griffiths, whilst the magnificent, dramatic sets were beautifully designed and painted by the art master, Harold Auty. These productions took up a great deal of time but I always had enough on my hands with my non-school activities

Windermere Grammar School rugby team. Author sitting second on left.

and felt unable to play in any of them.

In the run-up to Christmas a tradition had developed for the school to put on a play for the general public and in 1953 I was persuaded by the English teacher, C 'Dick' Barton, to act in *The House-master*. Being an all-boys school there was one serious and challenging problem of there being no girls to take the female parts so boys had to be drafted in. I was one of those boys. The reviews were kind to me and the remaining photographs showed me to be quite convincing as the leading lady. We played to full houses in St John's Rooms which the school had hired for the week. I enjoyed the acting and before I left school did so in two further plays, again as a woman.

The school was divided into three houses designated by a colour stripe on the school cap. These were named after prominent mountains which could be seen from the school and I was allocated to Fairfield with green as its colour whilst the remaining two were Scafell (Red) and Wetherlam (Blue). These houses were a source of competition between boys especially on the sports field where matches between them took place in athletics, cricket, cross-country and rugby.

Prior to September 1945 when the school was still operating as a conventional grammar school, there had only been two houses, Bowness and Windermere, the boys being allocated based on where they lived. The rivalry between the boys from the two villages was so intense that any competition between the two houses became barely controllable.

Colin Tyson, who joined the school in 1944, recalls the rivalry which on occasions bordered on violence and whilst this was manageable with the eighty or so grammar school pupils, once the school was enlarged the problem became really acute. Some of the longer established teachers were conscious that having houses named after the two principal villages only exacerbated the problem and in 1945 the headmaster wisely decided to replace the village names with those of prominent Lakeland mountains and increased the number to three. Colin felt this move led to a decrease in the animosity although the rivalry between boys from the two villages continued for some time.

One activity which was ideal for the house system was the annual school walk in the Lakeland mountains. These were held each year with the ascent of your own house mountain taking place every other year and in the intervening year climbing one of the other house mountains. These walks took place in the days before any sophisticated clothing existed; anoraks and even walking boots were beyond the expectations and pockets of the boys. Like Wainwright we walked in our jackets and our school boots. In the photographs of the events there are boys in their full school uniforms including the caps. They simply had no more appropriate clothes.

These mountain climbs were exciting and divided into a strenuous walk and a slightly easier one. My choice was for the strenuous one in order to show off my affinity for the natural terrain. The most memorable occurred in 1955, when my house climbed Scafell. It was a warm humid morning but in the course of the early afternoon the clouds began to build-up and the atmosphere became oppressive. Worse was to come as our teachers, with their wider experience of the mountainous conditions, began to urge us to hurry down off the hills into Langdale.

Alas, the changing weather was too quick for us. The day became as if it were night with the clouds blackening even further. The mother and father of all thunderstorms broke out with accompanying lightning of all shapes and sizes and with it, torrential rain and large, hard hailstones. One boy was struck by lightning which had bounced off a nearby rock and left him shaken but otherwise unhurt but the rest of the party were petrified. As we descended into the valley bottom as quickly as we could, the hailstones were hitting our soaked summer shirts and we paddled through inches of flood water from the overflowing becks. There was resulting damage throughout most of the Lake District with the road washed away in Troutbeck, whilst Ambleside and other villages experienced flash floods. It was a frightening experience and it brought home to us, what our teachers had warned us of, that the mountains might be beautiful and wonderful places but they could also be dangerous. They could change on a whim and must be treated with caution and respect. Over the years, I have climbed all the 'Wainwrights' five times and know the mountains well but I have never forgotten that experience.

The traumatic events on the mountains taught us a lesson but did not deter us from exploring our own district. Not living in the village of Bowness itself, a group of us were regarded as country cousins which brought us closer together. Our bikes were crucial to us as we pushed the boundaries of our neighbourhood wider. One such journey was the three or so miles southwards to Hill of Oaks where Roy's granny, Mrs Greenslade, lived. Hill of Oaks, together with the adjoining Blake Holme, was a large stretch of woodland sandwiched between the main road to Newby Bridge and the lake, adjacent to the scout camp at Great Tower.

This was fascinating because on 25 November 1911 it had been where the first British seaplane had taken off and landed on water. In local folklore it is often asserted that Wavell Wakefield, had made the first flight. Wavell Wakefield was a flamboyant character who became an MP, peer and England rugby international and, although during the First World War he joined the Royal Flying Corps, he had nothing to do with that first flight in 1911. The driving force of that initiative was his uncle, Edward Wakefield of Kendal. In a perceptive move he appreciated that at 49 he was probably too old to undertake all the strenuous flying and appointed Stanley Adams, a Rolls Royce engineer, as his test pilot. His main rival was Oscar Gnosspelius, a prosperous local businessman who was based on the opposite western shore of Windermere. Two additional competitors were the Bowness businessman, Cooper Pattinson, and local vicar, Rev Sidney Swann who lost all his money in his efforts and was forced to withdraw.

Both Wakefield and Gnosspelius realised that the critical problem for a successful flight was the floats. In turn they both independently formed a relationship with the local boat builders, Borwicks. It was the skill of the Bowness boat builders that designed and built the appropriately shaped floats which allowed Wakefield's hydro-aeroplane, as it was officially called, to take-off and land. The *Waterbird* won the competition when Gnosspelius crashed his plane before progressing to become Wakefield's chief engineer.

There was considerable opposition to the use of the lake for flying led by Beatrix Potter who lived on the western side of Windermere and Canon Rawnsley, one of the founders of the National Trust. They were unsuccessful in their protest and Edward Wakefield pressed ahead in finessing his seaplanes with the Admiralty keeping a close watch on the developments. There was a flurry of activity offering visitors pleasure flights from the lake and for a short period, planes reputedly delivering the Royal Mail to the Isle of Man.

Quite an industry was built up with two centres on Windermere, one at Cockshott, whilst the other was where the first flight had taken place at Hill of Oaks. Following the successful flight, the

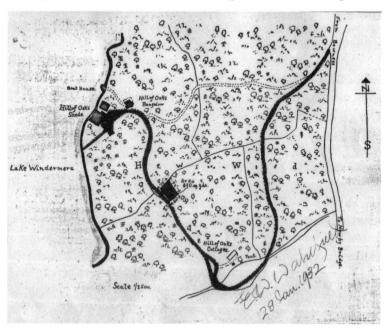

Map of Hill of Oaks area drawn by E W Wakefield, January 1932, with kind permission of the Lakes Flying Company Ltd.

First Seaplane 'Waterbird' over Windermere, 1911, F. Herbert, with kind permission of the Lakes Flying Company Ltd.

Lakes Flying Company was formed in 1911 but the first plane was destroyed in March 1912 when its hanger at Cockshott blew down in a gale. The hanger was at the southern end of the boatbuilding facilities and is now under premises owned by Aquatic Ltd. In 1914, the Northern Aircraft Company bought out the original company and diversified into providing flights for pleasure and training of pilots which caught the eye of the Admiralty. When the First World War broke out the Admiralty pursued its interest in using sea planes as a means of waging war and in 1916 the rural site was acquired by the Royal Naval Air Service and known as either RNAS Windermere or RNAS Hill of Oaks.

There had been considerable rivalry with somewhat of a frisson between the main proponents of the embryonic sea planes between Edward Wakefield, Cooper Pattinson and Oscar Gnosspelius. Fifty years on, one of our group, Mel, began working for Cooper Pattinson and heard at first hand details of the events surrounding those early flights. Cooper Pattinson claimed that he had made the first sea plane flight, taking off and landing, but it did not count as he was using a glider and not a powered plane. His glider was pulled off the lake's surface by a rope attached to a speed boat and with his specially designed floats he landed safely back on the lake.

Cooper Pattinson went on to have a successful career in the Royal Naval Air Service in the First World War at various stations but principally at Killingholme in Lincolnshire where he was the commanding officer. On 10 May 1918 over Heligoland Bight he shot down a Zeppelin from a newly designed flying boat and then discovered as he turned for home that one of his fuel pipes had been holed. He managed to land his plane on the rough sea and effected a partial repair which allowed him to limp home flying much of the way at only ten feet above the sea's surface. In order to judge how high his plane was above the sea he had been provided with a plumb line which he dropped from the cockpit. This he had found was very unreliable as the line was buffeted by the waves and wind and he had invented an alternative way of measuring the height. This involved fixing spotlights to the end of each of the wings and where they met gave the height which was a much safer way of flying at a low level. He was awarded the recently introduced Distinguished Flying Cross for his bravery following his escapades over the North Sea.

A descendant, Diana Matthews, told me how during the Second World War he had been invited to assist in adapting his ideas in the bombing of Ruhr Dams which were so critical to the German industrial production. These attacks in 1943 used Barnes Wallis's bouncing bombs which had to be delivered by aircraft flying exceptionally low. They proved to be effective with the dams being destroyed and became widely known to the British public by the release of the film, *The Dam Busters*, which was the most popular film of 1955. I can recall the great excitement locally when some of the filming was done over Windermere. We were absolutely thrilled to watch these wonderful planes droning up the lake at such a low altitude. In the film, the invention of the spotlight altimeters was incorrectly attributed to Guy Gibson and doubtless Cooper Pattinson had a wry smile on his lips as he watched the Lancaster Bombers flying over his 'home' lake. He was a legend in the Windermere area and we all knew him by sight but only Mel had intimate discussions with him.

Roy lived in one of the cottages on the Hill of Oaks estate and also in the adjacent Blake Holme Farm when his father was in the Far East during the war. He knew the area intimately. Much of the green areas and fields are nowadays being gradually lost to scrub and brambles but in the early fifties they were productive farmed areas amid the trees. He also remembered the location of the hut in which the sea planes were built and adapted. By the end of the Second World War it was being used by a local man for conventional boat building. Immediately in front of this building was a slipway by which the planes entered the water whilst next to this was a man-made flat piece of land which had a stone-built frontage onto Windermere. This was where the regular adaptations to the sea planes were made. It was simply called 'The Concrete' and remains intact and recognisable to this day.

Mrs Greenslade, Roy's granny, rented a sizable cottage near the lake and took in lodgers. Near her house were the original hanger and the slipway. It had a sizable industrial base initially belonging to the Lakes Flying Company. In a sense it seemed out of place in the middle of the rural area but we found exploring the remains of the industrial activity, half-hidden under trees, exciting and especially so in that many local people were unaware of what important work had taken place there. The industrial development was in two main stages, the first immediately following the successful flights at the end of 1911 and the second when the Admiralty requisitioned the area for the Royal Naval Air Service in 1916. A number of larger slipways were built as were some large hangers. Gradually over the years most of these larger developments fell into disuse and disrepair. Much of the infrastructure which supported the building of seaplanes and their operation has disappeared under the development of hundreds of holiday cabins. The importance of the activity is rapidly being forgotten as well as its importance to Britain in the First World War.

11
Flirting with Farming

Although we carried on playing in the outdoors and continued to be fascinated by nature, a subtle change had been developing for a while. We still wandered across the farmers' fields, and over the years I must have been in every field in a five miles radius of our homes. Over time however, we became increasingly interested in spending time on the farms themselves. We were growing bigger and stronger and better known to the local farmers. Jack Ellis of Bellman Ground and his workers knew us well. We got our milk from him and my father helped regularly when there was an excess of farm work, especially at hay time when I also began to help.

Increasingly we began drifting towards Bellman Ground and hanging around the farm. Jack Ellis had cows and sheep but it was the milking cows which demanded most attention. They were extremely labour-intensive, having to be milked twice a day, morning and late afternoon. Except in the most extreme weather, farmers still largely used the 'dog and stick method' of cow management which meant they were kept in the fields during the day and brought in for milking. Once inside, the cows inevitably became messy animals and one of the earliest tasks we were encouraged to undertake was the 'mucking out' of the cow byres. The handling of the cows took a lot of time and Jack Ellis realised that he could make use of the growing boys who were hanging around his farm and in turn we were delighted to help. It made us feel grown-up and doing something useful.

The cows' manure which we so assiduously cleared was stored for a period before being spread back onto the fields. In the earlier years, it was carted into the fields and either spread direct from the carts or dumped in small piles before being scattered wider by big curved forks. Eventually as tractors took over, a special muck spreader was acquired which made the task much easier. We may have thought this was solely a means of getting rid of the mountains of cow muck but it was also at the same time improving the composition and fertility of the soil.

We began assisting the regular farm workers bringing in the

Bellman Ground Farm

cows from neighbouring fields sometimes across the busy A592 to Barrow in Furness. Gradually, having gained Mr Ellis's confidence, we were allowed to drive them in ourselves. The cows were not milked by hand but by machine. Before this could happen however, the cows' teats needed to be washed and cleaned and then the milk must be seen to flow easily and this required each teat to be milked by hand for a few seconds. This was an acquired art involving squeezing and pulling the teat gently more or less at the same time and we learned how to do this.

There was a small period of danger in this process for the cows were tied in their stall and we had to take our stool and bucket towards the cow's rear end where there was always a chance of being kicked. It was important for the cow to get to know and accept you. Then there was much less chance of a kick. We were fortunate that most of the cows were Shorthorns or Ayrshires both of which tended to be reasonably placid although we had to careful of the Ayrshires as they had long dangerous horns. Over time we became proficient in the milking, not only enjoying it but also making ourselves useful and saving Jack Ellis money.

In those days, small farmers in the Lake District tried to be as self-sufficient as possible. Although the nature of the land lent itself primarily to livestock farming and wasn't ideal for arable, Jack Ellis grew some turnips and swedes which were fed to his livestock during the winter months. We also assisted in the thinning of the young turnips and then with their harvesting before transporting them back to the farm. They remained outside in a clamp covered with straw and soil which kept them safe from all but the most extreme of frosts. Another crop with which we helped was the growing of kale which was particularly nutritious for the cattle and saved the farmer from buying it in. An odd field of oats was even sown to provide cattle food and straw.

There was much else to do around the farm and we increasingly played a wider role. Jack was regularly asking us to look out for missing sheep on our wanderings over the fields. On many occasions, we would find them, often with their heads trapped in railings which we could release ourselves. The task was easier in that we knew the identification markings painted on the sheep which were specific to the individual farms. Gradually it just seemed natural for us to help generally whenever we were needed, even learning to drive the tractors in the fields which was a great thrill. When hay making came we were paid for assisting with harvesting the crop although naturally priority was given to the adults. But at least our abilities were being acknowledged. We also benefitted from being treated equally by Mrs Ellis who, when we returned to the farm with the hay, plied us with food she had prepared which was delicious. A further bonus came my way with his milk round which I had unsuccessfully tried to help with previously. Now, however, when he needed cover, he came to me for which I was paid.

Jack delivered his milk in a black Jowett van which was quite a popular choice for small businesses at the time. It was made by the Jowett company in Idle near Bradford between 1947 and 1953. It was relatively slow with a maximum speed of slightly over 50 mph being powered by a two-cylinder engine which resulted in it having a characteristic, and easily recognisable sound of 'pop-pop'. These Jowett vans were very economical, ideal for such tasks as milk delivery and popular in these years of austerity. I have never forgotten their characteristic sound.

By this time, we were all becoming quite accomplished and knowledgeable about work on the land and were probably making an unconscious assessment of whether we might do just that when we left school in the near future. We also attended talks and demonstrations at the Young Farmers Club at school. In addition, I had also made friends with Tommy Holliday, whose family farmed Barker Knott Farm next to Jack Ellis's, and for a period I spent quite a lot of time there, getting to know Tommy's slightly older brothers, Alan and Colin.

Bearing in mind I was the son of a local gardener and had shown considerable interest and knowledge of farming, I imagine that Jack Ellis would feel justified in encouraging me. On reflection, he did give me every opportunity to widen my experience on the farm. At the time it was probably a fair assumption that I would end up working on a farm for my living.

The year 1955 also marked the beginning of a period of change in my life. It almost seemed that the various activities which occupied so much of my time were coming together, in particular the widening of the role of the Youth Fellowship coupled with Alan Rayner becoming its leader.

Alan Rayner was always a most energetic man who was bursting with ideas for his own future and the lives of those with whom he was in contact. He was ambitious for himself and worked amazingly hard to achieve success which eventually did come. I first knew him in the late 1940s when he appeared in the district with a with an ex-army lorry. Together with a partner, Les Parker, he formed a timber business to help meet the demand for wood after the war. Although there was a plentiful supply of timber there was also much competition which proved very difficult for the new partnership to crack. They acquired a sawmill just a field away from Storrs Hall to which it had originally belonged and, although they struggled on manfully, it was a losing battle. The partners eventually were forced to go their separate ways with Alan retaining the sawmill and nearby fields.

In the field between the sawmill and Storrs Hall, I first saw an example of Alan's initiative and adaptability. The traditional Westmorland farming method of making hay was that after cutting, the hay was raked into piles to stand and dry before harvesting to the large haystack or barn. This drying stage was particularly difficult when the average annual rainfall could reach 100 inches. Alan had seen how farmers in equally wet western Norway coped with the problem and adopted their approach. Following the cutting of the grass, timber tripods 3-4 feet high were erected and the wet grass piled on them. The circulating air and wind aided the drying of the hay. It was the first example I had seen of his foresight.

In addition to timber, there was also a national shortage of eggs which Alan quickly recognised and bought hundreds of hens which he kept in his converted sawmill in deep litter conditions. By this time, he had a full-time job, with an animal feed company, Silcocks, driving around local farmers in a pick-up truck supplying their needs. Normally, this work pattern allowed him, with an early start and late finish to feed the hens, morning and early evening, and then collect the eggs. However, increasingly it wasn't possible for him to fit all this in with the demands of his full-time job. I knew Alan through the Youth Fellowship and the sawmill where he kept his hens was only a few hundred yards from where we lived at Garden Hill. To cope with the changing demands of his day-job, he asked me if I would look after his hens when needed.

It was easy for me for I was familiar with hens and really enjoyed the work. The demands on me increased to almost a daily requirement. I then asked Alan whether I could do the job every day and he jumped at the suggestion. I then realised I couldn't do this as well as my paper round and so after several years I gave it up. I was always grateful to have had the round and the money it provided which over the years had revolutionised my, and my family's, life. I was a little sad but as I was now in the fourth form at school, the paper round had provided me with the wherewithal to contemplate staying on into the fifth, whilst the hens could produce the means.

It turned out to be a wise choice for I gained wider experience for possible permanent work. I fed and kept an eye on the health of the birds, provided grit to ensure the eggshells were strong. Any eggs with a soft shell were no use owing to handling difficulties and I was permitted to take those home as they were perfectly good for eating. Regularly I had to clean out the dirty straw in which the birds lived but that extra work took place in the evening or at the weekend.

A little later the hens began to be phased out to be replaced by pigs. As had previously been the case with eggs, now there was an ongoing shortage of pork and Alan knew he could help satisfy the demand. My work became slightly different and more demanding. It was a question of feeding and cleaning but with no eggs to collect. There was however one new demand I had not envisaged! One day, the boss announced he was going to show me how to castrate the recently born piglets. I was supplied with a sharp razor and Alan showed me how to hold the squirming piglet make a slit with the razor in its lower underbelly, squeeze out the testicle and simply slit it off. Then, I wasn't to forget to treat the other testicle in a similar manner. It was as simple as that and I was ordered to try the operation several times. A week later I was instructed to castrate a further batch of piglets. I was hesitant to do so but had no option. I had learnt another skill but not one I ever wanted to use again!

As the months passed and my GCE O-level exams began to loom on the horizon, I decided that I was doing too much work outside school. My mock O-levels indicated that, with some effort, I had a fair chance of passing the real examinations six months later. I decided to part company with Alan, to concentrate on my school work whilst earning some cash by working for Tommie Lowden in the timber industry which I found more congenial and manageable. I had learned a great deal from working with Alan and by doing so had decided against the idea of working on a farm after leaving school.

In the early 1950s, when Tommie was attempting to establish his business he lived behind the church in Lowside where I delivered newspapers and I had come to know him. He obtained premises near the Hole in't Wall pub which had earlier belonged to George and Jobling who were coachbuilders. For a period they had diversified into making cars. They bought in the engines and chassis and then used their skills of traditional coach building to construct the wooden bodies for the cars. It is hard to imagine cars being built in Bowness but John McDougall remembers getting rid of half-completed car bodies when Tommie first moved into his new premises.

I had already done odd jobs for Tommie and when John McDougall left, he asked me to help him out in the school holidays which I gladly did. A little later Gerald Brear also helped Tommie in a similar manner for a few months between his leaving the sixth form in July 1957 until he began a permanent job at Windscale. It was a pleasure to work with Tommie who showed all the generous good nature of people from the North East. He would turn his hand to anything and worked extremely hard whilst expecting you to do the same which in any case came second-nature.

Tommie had started his business after a spell in the army, training bren-gun drivers in Windermere and he had fallen in love not only with a local girl but also the Lake District. He struggled initially but gradually as his reputation spread for doing a thorough job, a steady flow of work followed. He was working at the bottom end of the market which meant the returns were low. He had little capital and was always trying to improve his work base and equipment. I can still see him setting off to a job in the morning on his auto-cycle with a can of petrol hanging on one side of his handlebars and a bag of tools on the other. In addition, he had the remainder of his equipment tied to the back of the auto-cycle or on his own back. Auto-cycles were in themselves somewhat ungainly variants of a motor cycle with pedals. They were popular in the austerity years of post war Britain but did not stand the test of time with few surviving. To say that Tommie was overladen and ungainly was somewhat of an understatement.

Much of the work involved the felling of trees which meant much sweat. These were the days before chain saws. Any major sawing task had to be done with a cross-cut saw. This was a saw with a strong blade, approximately four or five feet long, with wooden upright handles at each end which required two people to use, one on each handle. It was hard work and cumbersome but the only means of felling large trees. To fell such a tree, then to strip it of its branches and use the cross-cut saw to cut the remaining trunk into manageable lengths, might take the best part of a day's work for two people. Today with the sophisticated machines the Forestry Commission use, the work can be accomplished by one person in literally two or three minutes. In the mid-1950s Tommie needed someone like myself to help him out and I was happy to oblige.

Work with Tommie was varied and hard but good fun. I still recall the chats we had over our dinner-breaks as we ate our bait of sandwiches and drank our tea from the vacuum flask with the cork squeezed into the neck encased with grease-proofed paper. In the early 1950s thermos flasks were far from the efficient ones we have come to know. The tea was little better than tepid after the morning break, but the conversation was always good and quite incisive. Many years later Tommie was still insisting that, even at this early stage of my life I had told him, my ambition was to become a Labour MP. I myself don't recall being so clear about my future although I was certainly aware of the social injustices facing people in Britain. Tommie would nevertheless be correct as he always maintained throughout his life that this conversation happened.

Tommie gradually built a successful and well-respected operation but it was always a one-man business. He moved his home and business to a former water mill at Gilpin Mill near Crook where he continued to live happily. It was idyllic as there was a considerable amount of land and unused buildings connected to the former watermill which he very quickly put to good use. When he died aged 85 in 2008, he was buried in the churchyard of the Holy Trinity Church at Winster. Following a touching service in the packed church, we all moved out to the interment where Tommie had provided a surprise. Perhaps we could have anticipated a cross made out of wood but his further commitment to wood, upon which his lifetime work had been based, surprised many of us present. Following his coffin being lowered into the grave, instead of having soil to sprinkle on the coffin, he had arranged for a heap of sawdust to be at hand to be thrown into the grave. I found this a particularly moving part of the ceremony and it was typical of Tommie to have thought of this.

The work was great experience and provided me with knowledge and skills which would help me in the future in more ways than I could anticipate. Together with looking after the hens and the pigs, coupled with the years spent around farms with cows and sheep ensured that I had a broad understanding of work on the land. Ironically, the more I was learning of work on the land the more I was having second thoughts. It was becoming clear that it wasn't for me.

Several of my school friends were leaving school and entering the world of work. A slightly older friend, David Richardson, whose family owned the village butchers for several generations, left to become an apprentice at Fells Ltd when he turned fifteen in January 1953. The company made the machine tools for the wood manufacturing industry in nearby Troutbeck Bridge. David left Fells when he was 23 to return to the family business of butchering. In these days prior to the emergence of supermarkets, there were four butchers' shops in Bowness with a considerable demand for them all.

Towards the end of 1953, the reality of the world of work came home to me indirectly when more and more of my friends began full-time work. In those years it was possible to leave school at fifteen and most of those who were not in the academic stream did so. One such individual was my good friend John McDougall who lived at Cleabarrow in a cottage the family had obtained the tenancy of just prior to the Second World War. His home was three miles from the village in a similar direction to mine and we often cycled back together and, like many young men, we talked a great deal. John was already very good with things mechanical which was ultimately recognised by the largest car repairer in Windermere, R N Smith, who offered him an apprenticeship. John left school on a Friday evening in November 1953 and began work the following Monday.

John Willan was another who became an apprentice at Fells. Although a year older than myself, he had been at the junior school with me and had passed his 11-plus the year before me and therefore was in the form above at Windermere Grammar School which he left early. He was a bright apprentice and when qualified travelled widely representing the firm, including to the USA. Tragically, he was killed one morning a few years later when cycling to work leaving a wife, Barbara, and his five year old daughter Julie. Another friend, Colin Rigg, who was in the same age group as John left school a few months after him to go to work as an apprentice at Isaac Braithwaites (Ibis) in Kendal. Like myself, he lived outside the village where his father was a chauffeur and gardener in a big house at Linthwaite above Storrs Park.

Ernie Fallowfield became apprenticed to a less usual trade, radio and television. Ernie had long had a personal bent for these interests. I can still recall him using rooms behind his home and above where we left our bikes, to practice his radio skills. In the days before transistors and integrated circuits, he made crystal sets which, especially in the evening, could receive broadcasts from all over the world. It seemed magic to us and Ernie shot up in our esteem by constructing such equipment. After gaining experience on finishing his apprenticeship, he left the village for some years and set up a radio and TV repair business in Dent on the Cumbrian/West Yorkshire border. One reason he left was the high price of houses in Bowness although eventually he was to return.

Apprenticeships in those days were a means of obtaining a skill which would usually guarantee a job for life with a decent wage. Apprentice trained workers were considered to be the cream of working people. The training was spread over five years and involved experience on the job supplemented with a carefully constructed course with nationally recognised examinations. The employers played a full part in the formal structure. The apprentices would attend the local technical college for one or two evenings a week which were supplemented by the employer giving them a day off work to attend college. Those from the Windermere area attended Allen Technical College in Kendal following courses leading to City and Guilds examinations which were highly regarded in the industry. During their years of training they were paid slightly less than the rate for unskilled young people but it increased by annual increments and of course once completed, the wage was higher. It was a well-structured form of training which ensured an adequate supply of skilled individuals to meet the needs of local industry and society.

Only two of my close friends took an alternative route and stayed on into the sixth form at Windermere Grammar School, Gerald Brear from the year above me and John Beckett who had been in my class at both the junior and secondary schools. In turn they were both to follow successful careers but it necessitated their having to leave the Bowness area. Neither returned to live in the village on their retirement.

Gerald had followed the science syllabus in the sixth form and in 1957 on gaining his A-levels he obtained a job at Windscale up the coast in West Cumberland. This was at the forefront of the world's nuclear industry with the first commercial nuclear electricity generating station having been opened there at Calder Hall in October 1956. This was an exciting challenge for him and he prospered and remained there all his working life. The siting of the nuclear industry there proved to be ideal for him. Gerald was an enthusiastic cyclist and would often ride to and from his home at Ghyll Head the forty miles or so to Windscale each week, an exposed and tough ride especially in winter. The alternative was a difficult journey by rail or bus often involving a detour by Barrow in Furness. Initially he stayed at a hostel in Holmrook which Windscale provided and then he returned home for the weekend.

His starting work at Windscale couldn't have come at a more traumatic time. A couple of weeks before he was due to start, it was discovered on 10 October 1957 that one of the two piles on the site was on fire, resulting in Britain experiencing its worst nuclear accident. The conventional view amongst the planners was that there was no need for additional protection on the structures. However thanks to Sir John Cockcroft who was leading the team responsible for their building, had over-ruled those opinions and insisted that filters were fitted to the top of each of the piles. This initially re-sulted in considerable resentment with the filters being nicknamed 'Cockcroft's Follies' although after the fire those words were never used again. The filter of the pile on fire captured a large proportion of potential emissions. I don't think we fully appreciated at the time how close we were from an absolute disaster. The bravery, way be-yond what could have been expected, was crucial in saving the day. Sir John Cockcroft was obviously one such individual but we should not forget Tom Tuohy, the reactor manager, who climbed up the piles on a number of occasions risking his life, and Terence Price, a physicist who was first to raise concerns about escaping emissions. Many others exhibited great courage.

Like most other people in Cumbria, I was reasonably reassured by the official announcements at the time, yet remained somewhat perplexed. They said there was nothing to worry about yet we saw farmers forced to pour their milk down the drain. It was all a bit confusing. Fifty years later, following my appointment to the Sel-lafield Board I learned how close we had been to disaster. If the filters had not been installed, in all probability the emissions would have resulted in the whole of Cumbria and much of the North of England being devastated with thousands killed. We were so lucky. This was the workplace into which Gerald cycled in his first weeks at work which was literally a baptism of fire but a place where he was to spend the following forty years or so of his life.

At the time there were reports that some high radioactive read-ings had been detected around the site but these did not mean much to the general public. It was almost thirty years later, in the after-math of the Chernobyl nuclear disaster of 26 April 1986, that some of the dangers began to be understood. Restrictions on sheep move-ment across Europe were imposed with particularly heightened ac-tivity in the Lakeland hills surrounding Sellafield. In the mid-1980s, I was contacted by two farmers from the area, Lou Howson, who farmed in Wasdale and Denis Holliday, from Egre-mont who were especially concerned. Both their farms were subject to sheep movement restrictions which increased their ongoing worry over radiation levels on their farms. Both had been con-vinced that over the years they had come across pockets of radioac-tivity.

The restrictions which continued for a number of years con-vinced them that they had been correct in their suspicions. They were certain that the authorities were themselves concerned that the Chernobyl radioactivity could fall on already contaminated pockets of Sellafield sourced radioactivity and possibly create additional problems. The area was certainly carefully monitored and scrutinised for months and years ahead.

John Beckett lived further up the village in South Terrace with his sister Jean. His father was a chauffeur in his early life to Beatrix Potter's mother and following her death, to a number of people including a Windermere GP, Dr Gerrard, before finally working for Borwick Boatbuilders undertaking general driving duties. His parents, as with all our parents, had a hard time with his mother doing the inevitable cleaning jobs in local big houses.

His mother came from a traditional Methodist family and in turn, John and Jean, went to the Methodist Church not far from their home at the top of the village. They therefore did not participate in the Youth Fellowship which dominated so much of my youth. Nevertheless in those years like the rest of us, he was strongly committed to Christianity although in later years he was to describe himself as a humanist.

John was in the same form as me at Windermere Grammar School and when I left at the end of the fifth form in 1956, he carried on into the sixth form, leaving two years later with his A-levels. On leaving, he went to work in Kendal Library where he began a course which would see him ultimately attain his professional qualifications in librarianship. He moved around the country gaining valuable experience including at University of Manchester Institute of Science and Technology and a number of different libraries before spending 26 years at the Merlewood Research Station near Grange over Sands. This was an important environmental research institute initially under the Nature Conservancy and later the Institute of Terrestrial Ecology and specialising in 'woodlands, soil and fauna of mull and mor'.

As 1955 drew on, the day was fast arriving when I would have to make a decision about what I was going to do after school. I had already given considerable thought to this. It was clear to me that my staying on at school had been a great financial strain to my mother and father and that was one of the key factors which had resulted in my having a paper round and later doing other jobs whilst still at school. By earning some money I felt I was doing something to ease the strain. My mother had made it clear that she felt I was bright and should stay on at school to do my O-levels. At the age of eleven she herself had been offered a place at a girls' high school in Sunderland but given her father's state of health following his discharge from the army in the First World War, she couldn't possibly accept. It was always a matter of regret to her and she was determined that the same shouldn't happen to me. My father was more laid back but basically went along with my mother's wishes and was proud of my ultimate academic achievements. I could have left school when I was fifteen at the end of the Christmas term in 1954 and followed my father and his forefathers in making my living from the land. That decision I had rejected but now had to make a choice. There was never any question of my staying on into the 6th form at school. I was leaving. That was non-negotiable.

New job opportunities were becoming available as the 1950s unfolded many of which seemed secure for life. One such opportunity was with the Fresh Water Biological Association at Ferry House on the west side of the lake in what had been the Ferry Hotel. Prior to moving to the new location, it had been based at Wray Castle, a few miles along the lake towards Ambleside. At the end of term in December 1955, Roy Shorrock, obtained employment there as a laboratory attendant. He too left school on the Friday and started work on the Monday morning on the wage of £3.3 shillings a week. The work was varied and normally out of doors, involving the collection of samples from the lake and local tarns which were taken back to the laboratories for analysis. He stayed there for eight years before leaving to join the police force in Barrow in Furness.

Any thoughts I had of doing farm work as a career had been abandoned as I realised there was little prospect of my ever getting a farm of my own. There seemed no point in pursuing this idea. Even at that young age, I recognised the frustrations ahead if I were to end up as a farm worker at the beck and call of an individual farmer. It seemed too reminiscent of my Dad's work experiences.

My experience working on the land however, did not prove to be in vain. In 1972, as a young MP for Colne Valley, I was appointed as the Shadow Minister for Agriculture, Fisheries and Food. When appointing me, the former Prime Minister, the Rt Hon Harold Wilson said I had a knowledge of agricultural matters almost unique in the Parliamentary Labour Party and that I could make a real contribution to the debates from the Opposition front bench. In the 1950s, I never would have anticipated that the knowledge I was gaining would be used in such august surroundings.

At the time I still wanted to work in the local area and to do so out of doors. In common with all my closest friends, I didn't want to work in an office 'sitting on our bottoms pushing a pen'. I knew the lake and enjoyed it. Working on research projects connected with it seemed to be right up my street. Talks with Roy had given me much more of an insight about what went on in Ferry House. In the approach to leaving school I had been exploring employment opportunities which included an interest in working for the Fresh Water Biological Association. Following an interview there, I had been made a provisional offer of a job providing I passed my GCE O-levels. I was happy as were my Mam and Dad. It appeared to be working out fine for my future and justified my staying on in the fifth form. All I had to do was to pass my exams. But I would have to wait until the end of August before I would know.

12

Into Permanent Work

As the mid-1950s loomed, a subtle change was occurring in my thinking although I wasn't conscious of it at the time. Along with my friends, I was becoming keener on cycling. I had various bikes but as I rode more I became increasingly particular about my 'best bike'. One thing I recall was the desire to obtain drop handlebars, derailleur gears and a frame made of 531 tubing which was particularly light. With my earnings from my paper round I saved sufficient money and bought a brand-new Hercules cycle for £26. This new bike made it much easier to undertake longer journeys.

Prior to this, I had been increasingly using my old bike for getting around the district. Then, in early 1956, my diary records me joining with friends to go on longer rides. Then after finishing with my paper round I had more time to get away on a Friday evening for much longer trips which entailed overnight stays at youth hostels. I even kept a record of these journeys.

At Easter 1956 I made my first tour with Frank Hantom who had been in my school year and was then doing an apprenticeship in engineering. We set off on Saturday and stayed at Gretna approximately sixty miles from home. The following day we toured the area between Dumfries and Kirkcudbright before riding home on Easter Monday. Each night we stayed in bed and breakfast accommodation costing around ten shillings (fifty pence in decimal money). Six weeks later, a few weeks prior to my sitting O-levels, Frank and I cycled across the Pennines over the course of three days, by way of Sedbergh, Hawes and Richmond, and stayed with my Aunty Dot in Darlington. We spent the Sunday cycling to Durham City where we were impressed by the grandeur of the majestic cathedral but surprised to find all the tourist shops closed. Then we rode across to Teesside taking in Stockton, Redcar and Middlesbrough before returning home the following day, Bank Holiday Monday having covered 250 miles.

These trips proved interesting and exciting but we decided that one way to improve them and reduce the cost was to join the Youth Hostel Association – subsequently we stayed at youth hostels. On

Author astride his new Hercules bicycle.

another trip with Frank the following August we stayed at youth hostels in Galloway which was a great success. In October I persuaded John McDougall and John Willan to join me for an overnight tour. We set off for Duddon in Furness, arriving there at seven o'clock only to find the hostel had burned down so we had to cycle over Wrynose Pass in the dark to reach the hostel at Elterwater. That was an unwelcome experience but it didn't deter us.

The following month John McDougall and Gerald Brear and myself set ourselves an even more arduous course visiting Chester, Shrewsbury, Wrexham, Llangollen returning over the Horse Shoe Pass and through the Mersey Tunnel, all in five days. We were becoming more confident of our abilities. In January of 1957, I showed even greater confidence when I set off alone on an overnight visit to Buttermere, Crummock Water and Loweswater in the northern Lake District before returning home by Whinlatter Pass and Keswick. Easter 1957 saw Frank Hantom and myself once more joining up for a four-day trip taking in Manchester, Buxton, Lincoln, Harrogate and the Yorkshire Dales. That trip marked the end of my cycling tours during which I had covered hundreds of miles and seen much of Northern England and Wales and Southern Scotland.

In my log book of tours, I wrote at Whitsuntide 1957, "have decided to have a bash at hitch hiking because in a limited time, we cannot see enough by cycling." Our very first attempt at hitch hiking exceeded our wildest expectations. Frank and myself set off on the A6 from Kendal and our first lift was in a car travelling to Inverness with the driver, who turned out to be a vet who was wanting company for the 300 mile journey. I don't think we ever had a lift which bettered that first attempt at 'thumbing'. We only had three days for the trip and on the second we journeyed along the Moray Firth and down to Perth by Aberdeen. Then on our final day we left Perth Youth Hostel arriving home late in the evening at eleven o'clock. We had perhaps been spoiled but we didn't recognise that. I summarised our feelings, "Had such good lifts. I don't think we will go on many cycling tours for a while now". For me that turned out to be the case.

At the end of July 1957, I set off alone for a trip to Ireland. I spent two weeks hitch hiking around both the north and south of the island, visiting Belfast, Dublin, Cork, Killarney, Limerick, the Giant's Causeway and the Mountains of Mourne before sailing back from Larne. On one leg of the trip I was picked up on a pony and trap, a unique experience for me. The Irish people were so hospitable and by staying at youth hostels I was never short of company.

The following month saw me hitch hiking with a work colleague, Albert, this time visiting London. It went like clockwork and we spent three full days enjoying the many sights of the capital city. We were both enthralled and I wrote in conclusion, "My first visit to London but I am sure not my last." This was more prophetic than I realised at the time.

At Easter and Whitsun 1958 Roy Shorrock joined me for two trips to Central Scotland which had an ulterior purpose. Roy and I were already planning to attempt something 'really big' and these Scottish trips were in anticipation of our summer holidays. What we had in mind was to hitch hike around Northern Europe. There was a great deal of preparation needed such as getting our passports, planning our route, buying suitable travelling clothes and adequate footwear. The latter were ex-army boots with thick rubber soles which I wore for years afterwards in completing the 214 Wainwright summits in the Lake District. In the days when travelling abroad was unusual, this was to be such a big adventure and we were determined to prepare properly.

To maximise the time available Roy travelled down to meet me in Lancaster and we set off hitching at six o'clock and travelled overnight to London. After some very brief sightseeing we were quickly on our way again to Dover to catch the morning boat to Calais. Once the excitement of being abroad for the first time had waned we were slightly concerned whether we would get lifts in France. We need not have worried and spent our first night in the youth hostel at Lille. From there we moved on through Belgium and stopped in Brussels to visit the World Fair which was in the city that year. From there we departed for Holland to be enthralled by the canals, windmills, small fishing villages with the locals in national dress including their wooden clogs. We moved through Germany to Bremen and Hamburg before striking north to Denmark and Copenhagen. Our stay was brief before we caught a ferry to Helsingborg in Sweden which was the furthest north we could travel because of time constraints. It was then back to Germany, down the Rhine Valley to Luxembourg and finally to France and the ferry back to England.

It was truly a whistle-stop tour. In sixteen days we visited six countries and hitched about 3,000 miles. We rarely had difficulty in getting lifts and met nothing but friendliness and a genuine welcome everywhere. Outside Germany, where the people were most hospitable, we were constantly reminded that Britain had liberated their countries in 1945 a mere thirteen years previously. When an account of our travels appeared in the *Windermere Parish Church Magazine* the following November, the editor described our visit as, 'a most adventurous journey through six European countries by two members of our Youth Fellowship. We congratulate them on their spirit of adventure and enterprise.' Thankfully that spirit of adventure continues, albeit slightly less ambitious, when Roy, Mel and myself walk the Lakeland fells every Friday.

Looking back, I can now see that my life was beginning to change. It is surprising that the initial overnight trips were in the weeks leading up to my O-levels in June 1956 suggesting that I was supremely confident, which I wasn't. I had a strong desire to travel. I don't recall swotting for the exams except taking a rowing boat

Storrs Temple, Windermere.

136

out on the lake and laying in the boat bottom reading my notes with occasional glances up to the iconic fells of Fairfield Horseshoe and Claife Heights. In the mid-1950s, the tourist season started later and the lake was much quieter with only the large white steamers making waves big enough to shake my small boat. There were five such vessels: MVs *Swan, Teal, Swift, Tern* and *Cygnet* which were owned and operated by British Rail.

Earlier in the twentieth century, when the lake was used more as a transport route, there was a sixth vessel, the *Raven*, which was used to carry goods and luggage but by the 1950s this was no longer operating. In the earlier period the steamers landed at a number of the prominent lakeside hotels which had their own large piers. Up until the mid-sixties following the Beeching Report on the railways and the closure of the line from Ulverston to Lakeside, the official rail route to Bowness from the south was by that line and completed by boat. When Pat, later John McDougall's wife, travelled from Preston to Bowness for a job interview in the early 1960s, she made her journey by this route on the advice of British Rail.

One of these disused steamer piers, the one at Storrs, has proved to be a continuing bone of contention to those who lived nearby. The problem remains unresolved well into the twenty-first century. The locals claim they had a right of access which had gone unchallenged for decades. For seventy years to my knowledge this access has been an issue with no sign yet of its resolution. The problem is further accentuated by the presence of Storrs Temple, a Grade Two listed building, adjacent to where the pier had been. This edifice sticks out into the lake and is accessed via a short stone pier. It was built in 1804 and is described in its listing as, "Octagonal, stone with cornice. Four open round arches, and four tablets to admirals Duncan, Nelson, Howe, and St Vincent." To make the issue more sensitive the structure is owned by the National Trust. The traditional access to the Temple was by the disputed route.

At that time I wanted to travel more widely and see other parts of Britain and ultimately, Europe. Until I did so, my experience of Britain was limited to the four northern counties of England, Cumberland, Durham, Northumberland and Westmorland, and Dumfries and Galloway across the border in Scotland. This desire was shared by my friends and represented a marked change from our previous commonly held views that we wanted to spend our lives in the Windermere area.

As a result of our travelling we not only gained knowledge but perhaps just as important, confidence. As young people living in a small self-contained village we were rather diffident, living in awe of those of our own age who lived in towns and cities. These boys seemed more sure of themselves and some of them even had steady girlfriends, something we often spoke of amongst ourselves but rarely acted upon. These cycling and hitch hiking experiences certainly taught me that I could confidently deal with most problems. In fact, half way through this period I had already taking the first steps of moving away from Bowness.

At the end of June 1956, with the O-level examinations behind me and although still technically a schoolboy, I found a new temporary job whilst waiting for my results when, hopefully I would begin working with Fresh Water Biological Association at Ferry House. Tommie Lowden had told me that he could not afford to continue employing me on a full-time basis and suggested I approach the forestry company, Mould and Bloomer whom he had heard were on the lookout for workers. The firm was well established and successful. I duly applied and following an interview with the proprietor, Archie Galloway, at their offices above Martin's Bank on Royal Square, Bowness, was offered and accepted a job. All was falling into place.

There had been one half-hearted attempt at school to persuade me to stay on. Mel Jeffrey, who was leaving school at the same time as myself, had obtained a final interview with the headmaster, Stanley Lewis, and persuaded me to accompanying him. He knew the head better than me having sung alongside him in the school choir and played with him in the school orchestra. I don't recall ever having a one to one with the head in the previous five years although he had taught me maths. At the interview, he suggested that I should stay on at school. A suggestion I summarily dismissed. It reinforced my view that he simply had no empathy with ordinary working people and no notion of the financial pressures on low-paid working families of sons or daughters staying on at school. Towards the end of July, I had lined-up a temporary job on the assumption I had passed sufficient O-levels, then I would begin working permanently in September for the Fresh Water Biological Association as a scientific civil servant.

In July 1956, thousands of miles away, as I was leaving school, President Nasser of Egypt nationalised the Suez Canal causing great

Author in Germany hitchiking, 1958.

consternation in the West and particularly in Britain and France both of whom used the canal for so much of their trade. The act of seizing the canal caught the allies by surprise and rather belatedly in October 1956, Britain, France and Israel led an ill-fated military invasion of Suez. Throughout the summer and early autumn, Anthony Eden's Conservative Government had been unsuccessfully trying to build a political consensus whilst preparing for military action. As part of this process, government civilian spending was reined back including a freeze on new civil service appointments.

At a stroke, everything changed, resulting in my carefully worked-out plans falling apart. A message came from Ferry House that they were having to withdraw their provisional offer in line with the Government's new economy measures. It was difficult to appreciate that my personal future was being directly affected by the knock-on effects of an international decision by the President of Egypt. It was so unexpected and hard to take. It was an early lesson of the consequences of politics at the highest level affecting ordinary people going about their day to day business – even a simple school leaver. That was that and I had to accept it. During my short life, I had already observed that this was the lesson working people had learned to accept over the generations.

I was informed of this disappointing news as I was about to travel to the North East of England for the family's annual weeks holiday. It proved to be a somewhat difficult time for both myself and my parents. The high point of the week for me was to again see Darlington AFC play a game of professional football but at the back of my mind was my exam results for which we were still waiting.

On our return home and having pushed open the front door, there on the floor was the buff stamped addressed envelope which I had left at school for my results to be sent. Clutching the envelope, I went outside the porch into the open air with Mam and Dad alongside me. I ripped open the envelope, pulled out the sheet of paper to see that I had passed all the six exams I had taken. My mother hugged me as, rather unusually, did my dad. There it was in black and white, I had O-levels in English Language, Mathematics, Geography, History, Latin and French. It couldn't have been better and it justified my having stayed on at school. Everyone was delighted. On reflection, I felt a little down hearted that I wasn't seen fit to work for the government at the Fresh Water Biological Association. I knew from observation that crying over spilt milk got you nowhere and I simply had to accept the situation and get on with it. At least I had a job in forestry which I had started and was thoroughly enjoying. It was challenging but rewarding.

Ironically, in my new job I travelled past the headquarters of the the Fresh Water Biological Association at Ferry House every morning as I cycled to Mould and Bloomer's nurseries at Harrow Slack which were a mile or so northwards along the lake shore. I left home at about 7.10am to catch the ferry across the lake twenty minutes later. The ferry in those days was rarely late. It was powered by steam and Roy's father had the job of wheeling the coke onto the vessel to power the boilers. Mould and Bloomer employed twenty or so people and I began working for them, learning the ropes at their nurseries before going out with one of the two working gangs.

Following my induction in the nursery, I was attached to a group of fellow workers on a project clearing, fencing and then planting small trees or slips near the summit of Claife Heights on the western side of the lake. Once more this entailed catching the ferry at

7.30am and cycling a further three miles, up a very steep hill, before leaving our bikes, struggling up the fellside whilst carrying our tools and young trees. It was a hard slog and took over half an hour to get to where we were to begin work. We persevered with the preparatory arrangements and planted the trees most of which survived and I saw prosper over the years. These were only slips of trees which we carried in a hessian bag on our backs. We followed a very straightforward planting process. We walked backwards and with a mattock, which is a type of pick axe with one flat blade, and cut a V shape in the soil into which we inserted the slip of a tree before heeling it in as we moved onto the next planting. Our productivity was surprisingly high and on a good day each of us could plant over a thousand trees.

Once this job was completed, we then moved on to a contract with the Forestry Commission to plant up much of Chapel Woods near Staveley in Cartmel. This did not involve another ferry journey but we had to cycle five miles down the hilly A592 towards Newby Bridge where we left our bikes and again set off to walk up the fellside to the Forestry Commission planting sites. This was a major contract for the firm and sixty years later, with a computer-controlled machine costing tens of thousands of pounds, I felled some of the trees I had planted. It took only two or three minutes to complete the task which would have taken a full day's work sixty years previously. It felt very significant to have harvested a tree which I had planted and it brought home to me the long term nature of forestry whilst making me realise how fortunate I was to have witnessed the results of my earlier efforts. During my adult years the twelve-inch slip had grown into a 70 foot tree – the magic of nature with just a little help from a human!

Following that I was moved to work nearer home and planted trees in Blackbeck Wood where I had played as a child when my father worked at Broad Leys. That only involved a bike ride of minutes – a mere doddle. I had a new foreman on this job, Bill Cottam, who was well into his fifties. He had served in the Border Regiment throughout the First World War and survived. Not surprisingly he was somewhat hesitant and slow in his approach with the result that we younger ones never fully made allowances for what he had been through. To this day I still regret that.

As I came to learn what Bill Cottam had been through during the First World War, in the mud of the trenches of the Western Front

141

and seeing the carnage all around, with his friends and colleagues dying in agony, I came to regret our attitude. He, like so many of his generation, rarely spoke of the experiences. It made me realise how important learning and knowledge is to the way we live and behave. Bill had never left the area until the army took him across the sea to Belgium and France but then he was to return to Windermere with those horrible memories. Perhaps planting trees in harmony with nature helped him to come to terms with what he had been through. I hope so. In modern times this would be called a therapy but Bill would have seen it as simply a job which allowed him to earn a living. I still feel humbled in the thought of what a good man he was.

I went on to work with him for several months and sadly some time later he was killed in a motorcycle accident on the outskirts of Bowness. It happened after he had finished a day's work in the nursery and had travelled back on the ferry with a work colleague, Rod Owen who was on his push bike. They said their goodbyes and parted. Rod followed the same route a few minutes later only to discovered Bill lying dead beside his motorcycle. It was never established what precisely had happened but he at least died in his beloved Lakeland and not in the mud and chaos of France.

There was one other First World War veteran with whom I came in contact. He lived near us with Harry Atkinson's family in Storrs Cottages opposite Rayner's sawmill. Each day, he walked into Bowness to work and all the time talking to himself. It was common knowledge that he had seen active service during the First World War and suffered severely from shell shock. Thankfully we never made fun of him for we never spoke with him. Indeed, there was a rather comical side to our relationship. He worked in the small shop and hairdressers opposite the church in Bowness which Harry Atkinson owned. Our bus stop home was immediately outside the shop and naturally we had our hair cut there. We boys were invariably directed to the former soldier to our dread. His hands shook uncontrollably at times and as he used manual clippers, he would jerk bits of our hair out. Our hair looked as if it had been nibbled by rats after a bad dose of Mr Miller. It really hurt and looking back it is quite amusing but we didn't think so at the time.

As 1956 drew to a close, my work with Mould and Bloomer moved away from the vicinity of Windermere. They had won a contract to plant up a large tract of land on Lord Shuttleworth's estate in the most northern extremity of Lancashire. The family could trace its origins back to the cotton industry and to the socially reforming family of Kay. They had always been closely identified with Lancashire and traditionally had lived at Gawthorpe near Padiham until moving to Leck Hall.

A handful of us younger employees were encouraged to volunteer for this project as it was not attractive to the married men. It was too far to travel daily so we were provided with accommodation at the Red Lion Hotel in Kirkby Lonsdale during the week. I found this quite exciting as it was the first time I had stayed in a hotel which seemed luxurious to me. It entailed cycling over twenty miles there on a Sunday evening for an 8am start on Monday morning and then on each workday we had to make the ten mile round trip from hotel to workplace. Both rides were arduous on hilly roads but fortunately we were all accustomed to travelling such terrain on our bikes. Routinely, the travel to Kirkby Lonsdale would be on a Sunday evening with the return after work on Friday.

Leck Hall was situated just outside the village of the same name which itself was a few miles north of Cowan Bridge, a village on the main A65 road between Kendal and Skipton. Cowan Bridge's main claim to fame is that it was where the Brontë sisters attended school and Charlotte had used her experiences there very graphically in *Jane Eyre*. The large estate in question occupied a narrow finger of land squeezed between Cumbria and West Yorkshire and crucially for the Shuttleworth family was in the County of Lancashire. This was important to the aristocratic family as it enabled them to remain eligible to hold the prestigious post of Lord Lieutenant of Lancashire, which the current Peer holds. The family has always remained intensely proud to hold this title and takes its responsibilities as representative of the Queen very seriously indeed.

Forty years later, this experience resulted in an amusing incident. I was appointed as Chancellor of the Duchy of Lancaster in Tony Blair's Cabinet of 1997. The formal installation was conferred by Her Majesty in person and subsequently we had regular one-to-one meetings to discuss Duchy business. On one of these occasions, Her Majesty inquired in passing whether I knew Lancashire well, to which I replied one of my earliest jobs was planting trees on the estate of her Lord Lieutenant, Lord Shuttleworth. She smiled, was clearly amused, and replied instantaneously, 'My word, the wheel really has turned, hasn't it?'

The tree planting at Leck was on the foothills of the Pennines and the terrain was less rocky and steep than the Lakeland fells with the result our rate of planting increased. The wind however was often persistent and it could be unpleasantly cold in those early winter months but we probably planted for a few additional weeks than we could have done nearer home. It broadened my experience and helped in convincing me that a life working in forestry would be very acceptable and enjoyable.

Furthermore, the work would often be in some of the most beautiful parts of the country. I had already determined that forests were too important to be left solely to the foresters and landowners. I was convinced that trees and forestry brought more than economic benefits to the nation having vital conservation, environmental and recreational benefits. This wasn't a universally held view at the time. I could understand the landowner holding proprietorial views but was at a loss when forest workers sometimes felt likewise. Thankfully, views have changed. In 1986, I successfully promoted an environment act which required the Forestry Commission to take into account environmental factors in addition to forestry objectives. Then 50 years later as Chair of the Forestry Commission, I took great satisfaction in declaring that freedom of access on foot would be guaranteed by law on all Forestry Commission freehold land.

I was conscious that if I was to follow forestry as a career I ought to obtain appropriate professional qualifications. As I began to explore the possibility, it was clear to me that the state-owned Forestry Commission might not only provide me with a secure job but also offer opportunities to achieve such formal qualifications. In 1956 the Forestry Commission had a much more extensive role than it does today. It employed thousands and was the largest landowner in Britain – the latter is still true in the third decade of the twenty-first century.

Several universities had forestry departments offering degrees in forestry. These courses were out of my reach as I did not have the requisite entry qualifications of A-levels. The Forestry Commission however seemed to offer a way forward. To ensure sufficient qualified forest workers and managers it had formal training schemes including its own colleges which provided full-time courses of two years for selected individuals to gain forestry training and to become potential management material.

In the early 1950s the Forestry Commission ran five of these

Forestry Training Schools. I discovered I had the necessary entry qualifications and in late 1956, I sent off an application and was excited when I had a reply accepting me onto a course. The excitement waned when I read on to discover there was a wait of five years before a vacancy would occur. At the age of seventeen, this seemed a lifetime away and after a deal of discussion and even more thought, I decided that I did not want to wait that long. I decided against a career with the Forestry Commission although I was to retain a lifelong interest in forestry. Eventually forty years later in 2001, I did join the Forestry Commission as its chairman. I remain proud to have been the first forestry worker to achieve that role. With hindsight perhaps I took the right decision at seventeen!

During the process of applying to the Forestry Commission for a training place in 1956, I felt that I needed an O-level in a science subject other than mathematics. As was the case for many young people living in a rural area, I found that even the local college at Kendal did not offer an O-level evening course in a science subject. The nearest I discovered was in Lancaster, thirty miles away. I had decided on chemistry as my subject and my only way to do the course, like thousands of other rural dwellers, was by a correspondence course. This form of remote learning was not easy and I have the highest regard for those who gain their qualifications by this means. It is a lonely and isolated process and without any direct verbal contact with a tutor makes it tricky. Not being able to ask a simple question directly to someone, makes the courses difficult, but for me it was the only way forward. My close friend Mel Jeffrey found himself in the same predicament when his employer refused him any time off to attend a professional course at the local Kendal College. His only means of gaining a qualification in quantity surveying was by a correspondence course.

In those latter months of 1956, I was once again wrestling with what I should do as a career. I had my whole life before me. In spite of my original intentions of working out of doors and doing so in South Lakeland, I was beginning to re-assess the situation. My comfort zone was widening as my O-level passes and my cycling tours had given me self-confidence. I was realising that in spite of the assumption of some in authority, I actually had some potential.

Throughout my short life and I guess this was the same for my friends, no-one considered us as anything other than 'the hewers of wood and drawers of water' for society. Especially at Windermere Grammar School, some clearly took this view. Many had failed to appreciate that the war had changed things. Victory on the battle-field had moved onto a battle for the type of society which was re-quired in post-war Britain. Those who had fought in the war had clearly indicated what they expected when they voted in such large numbers for Attlee's Government in 1945.

Life in the countryside was somewhat different from that in the urban areas. In political terms it was not too far removed from being feudal. In later years, a number of my parents' friends who worked for the 'big house' confided in me that they had always voted Labour but had never dared tell anyone in case their employ-ers found out. That was certainly the position in my home. Bow-ness society was not anything like as feudal as in even more remote rural areas, but with trade unionism being weak and collectivisation alien to the way of life, the individual's struggle for change and to attain some self-esteem was often a lone battle.

With my experience widening as I saw more of Britain, I began to view my future employment in a different light. I felt certain that science was the key in the future. I learned of a vacancy as a labo-ratory assistant at Lansil Ltd at Lancaster and applied. The com-pany was a modern textile company at the forefront of developing man-made fibres, employing 3,000 people. I was successful and commenced work there in February 1957. I finished working in forestry on a Saturday morning and the afternoon of the following day saw me packing my meagre belongings into my saddlebag and rucksack, and riding off to my new place of work.

In many respects Lancaster was an ideal testing ground. It was the nearest recognisable industrial city, yet only thirty miles from Bowness and although I might be working there, I could easily re-turn home if I wished. I may have been working in industry in the city but my home and principal friendships remained rooted in the Lake District. In later years when the M6 motorway was com-pleted, I could easily have commuted daily but in 1957 that was not viable.

My new job was as a scientific apprentice which unfortunately had the disadvantage that my monthly wage was less than I had been getting in forestry but I knew with careful planning I could just about get by. I recall often on the last weekend of the month I would be scrimping just to get by. I cycled the thirty miles to

Lancaster each week which meant saving on bus or train fares whilst helping me retain my fitness. I was fortunate in getting digs about a mile or so from work with a lovely couple, Dick and Sarah Carradus who lived in a terraced street, Gregson Road, where they ran a corner shop near the renowned Lancaster Grammar School.

Dick's day job was as a coach painter but he assisted Sarah with the running of the shop. In any spare time he loved distance running. He was known throughout the district as the mainstay of running in the city, being not only an officer of the City of Lancaster Harriers but also at the ripe old age of over 50 still an active participant, although as he would freely admit he was somewhat past his prime. However, what he may have lacked in speed he more than made up in dedication. It was this enthusiasm that persuaded me to join him and take up running which did wonders for my fitness. Only a few years previously, I had been required to undertake the senior set-run at school so had some experience at cross-country running and usually had acquitted myself reasonably well.

As I became more established in the harriers, I was chosen to represent the City of Lancaster in the county, regional and ultimately the national cross-county championships, albeit not with any great success. These were the days before half-marathons and the like had become fashionable but I did participate in a number of other races including the Windermere to Kendal Road Race alongside the former world champion and Olympic medal winner, Derek Ibbotson, of Huddersfield. Admittedly I hardly saw him after the start! I enjoyed the running experience and it helped keep me fit for football.

Initially, work at Lansil was more of a culture shock than I had anticipated. It was strange working inside and being oblivious of the weather. Every morning at 8.30am I had to clock-in and then for eight hours I was inside before clocking out, but I quickly adjusted. There were a number of young people with whom I became friends and they showed me the ropes. Everyone was friendly and helpful. Basically, the job in the laboratory was to check the company's final products as part of the quality control process coupled with the more specific task of taking samples of the incoming raw cotton to judge its suitability for the manufacture of man-made fibres.

The company was progressive and deemed it important that, as scientific apprentices, we developed the necessary skills for our profession. In pursuit of this I was required to attend Lancaster Technical College on a three-year course leading to an Ordinary National Certificate which with a further two years study could be converted to a Higher National Certificate. It was an onerous challenge with Lansil giving us a day off each week to attend classes which were then supplemented by our attending an additional two evenings a week in our own time. It was a well-constructed course leading to a recognised qualification and cadre of well qualified staff.

Whilst I took my work responsibilities seriously and quickly acclimatised to my new living conditions, the bulk of my social activities remained in Bowness. The distance was such that it was feasible for me to cycle back home on a Friday after work and return on a Sunday evening or even a Monday morning in the summer. It might be thought that I was a part-time member of my group in Bowness but that was not the case. I missed very little of what was happening for we were all now working, with a number of us, attending night classes, with the result that there was little activity on weekday evenings. I was still regarded as a Bowness lad.

Things began to change during the winter of 1958/9. With extra money from my annual increments and working anti-social hours, I began to travel on the express bus to Lancaster which left Windermere at 6.30 on a Sunday evening. Admittedly the journey was slow for the motorway had not then been opened north of Lancaster with the journey down the A6, calling at most of the towns and villages, taking almost two hours. The bus was heavily used by young people who were returning from their Lakeland homes to where they had found work in Lancashire and over the months I began to make new friends.

Meanwhile our social life in Bowness was regular and predictable. We increasingly visited local pubs and took a drink on the weekend evenings. Our favourite pub was the John Peel, immediately next to the parish rooms, or sometimes we'd visit the Stags Head or the Hole In't Wall. Very occasionally, we might go to the Hydro which was regarded as a bit posh. On Saturdays, a drink or two in the pub, would be followed by a visit to the local dance at the Palace.

The dances at the Palace were almost an institution amongst the young people of South Lakeland who flocked to them from miles around. It was simply the best. The Palace was situated in North Terrace in Bowness above the Soldiers and Sailors Club where my father would be having his weekly pint with Ted Shorrock. The music was provided live by the Baronettes which included Mel on either the clarinet or saxophone. We were becoming increasingly interested in girls and the Palace proved to be the ideal place to meet a wider cross section.

The traditional dance on New Years' Eve was the one to which we most eagerly looked forward. Not only did it attract many additional dancers but when the clock struck midnight, the young men and women, would embrace, kiss and wish each other 'Happy New Year'. In many cases, it was the nearest we got to being intimate with girls.

During these years the influence of the church was still there but diminishing amongst most of my friends including myself. Our voices had broken several years previously and we were no longer in the choir, although the Youth Fellowship under Alan Rayner's leadership continued to cater for our social interests. Visits to St John's in the Vale remained popular and Alan acquired small premises below the Crown Hotel which he converted into a permanent meeting place for the Youth Fellowship but unfortunately it was not to prove successful in the longer term. Attendance at

St Johns in the Vale, May 1955, left to right Gerald Brear, Miriam Thornborrow, Norman Askew, David Clark and Julie Evans.

Evensong continued with the subsequent strolls along the promenade followed by long discussions in the shelters dotted along our walks. Although we didn't recognise it at the time, 'times they were a-changing'.

Meanwhile back in Bowness some of my friends were buying cars. In the mid-fifties, pre-war small cars were relatively cheap. The perceived cost of motoring depressed the market and meant that working families rarely considered the prospect of car ownership. The matter was aggravated further when a shortage of petrol followed the Suez Crisis in 1956 resulting in petrol rationing. This grabbed the newspaper headlines but did not permanently deter the ambitions of the younger generation.

It wasn't really a surprise that the first to get their own cars were the two Johns, McDougall and Willan. They were both apprentices in engineering and fascinated by things mechanical. John McDougall was even serving his time in a garage. Furthermore, living outside the village and having a car made life more comfortable and considerably easier for him. They both went for Austin 7s built in the mid-1930s although John Willan had a slightly larger vehicle. I would hazard a guess that they would have paid between £25-30 for them.

Then a third member of our group joined them, Colin Rigg. His needs were slightly different. He too lived outside the village and had begun an apprenticeship in the drawing office of Ibis, an engineering company in Kendal. To make travel to work easier, he bought a more modern and reliable vehicle, a Bond Mini-car. This was a revolutionary type of car built in nearby Preston. It was a three-wheeled car with the single wheel at the front and powered by a Villiers two-stroke engine. It had three forward gears but no reverse. This vehicle provided a reliable means for Colin to go about his business and crucially to get to work.

Their decisions induced others of us to join them with David Richardson leading the way by buying a pre-war Standard Nine saloon, popularly known as a 'Flying 9'. Over the years, my work in the textile mill had seen my wages increase and I began to feel a little better off. Then, having to work nights, resulted in a further wage increase. In the summer months I could supplement my income further by working in gardens at home in Bowness. Whilst living in Lancaster during the week I began to take some driving lessons for which my experiences of driving a Ferguson tractor several years previously, came in very useful in passing the driving test. I was drifting towards car ownership.

The die was cast in 1957, when someone at work at Lansil approached me with the offer of a car which I found irresistible. It was a BSA car with an open top and four seats which had been built in 1936. It was in its way, a somewhat revolutionary car being built largely of aluminium, having a front wheel drive, and with a gear change situated under the dash board. To cap all this, it was a striking bright red.

I paid my £25 and drove it back to my digs. My landlord Dick was duly impressed but felt it needed a new canvas hood and required repainting. He then offered to make a new hood and repaint the car at cost price. Knowing not to stare a gift horse in the mouth, I accepted his offer immediately and before long drove back home to Bowness in what appeared to be a spanking 'new' car. It looked stunning and my friends were impressed. I enjoyed my new toy and it provided a means of transport to and from Lancaster as well as around the Lakes although some of the steeper passes required much gear-changing and considerable perspiration, even on occasions needing any passengers to get out and push!

The 1936 BSA car.

Living in a rural area with public transport leaving a lot to be desired especially in anti-social hours, made car-ownership attractive. Before long other friends followed our lead. Frank Hantom bought a delightful convertible Morris Eight which, although built in the late 1930s, proved to be most reliable. In the summer of 1959, I joined Frank for a holiday touring the Highlands of Scotland and North East England. Roy Shorrock had acquired a pre-war Ford Popular and then Mel Jeffrey capped us all by obtaining a red MG two-seater sports car which cut quite a dash.

I thoroughly enjoyed my BSA which gave me so much fun, thanks occasionally to John McDougall using his recently acquired skills at work to effect repairs when I had pushed the old car just that bit too hard. I well recall him spending hours at Meadowcroft replacing the big-ends in the engine. It would have cost me the earth if a garage had done it. After a couple of years, I sold the car and bought another BSA for £10 but this time it was a 125cc motorcycle which had previously been used to deliver telegrams for the Post Office. It too was bright red. My pushbike took a back seat after many years of service. I began to feel I had come quite a way and that life was looking up.

13
Another Change at Home

As my own future employment had again become unclear, events were also happening with my father's job. The marriage of his employer's daughter, Marion, had seemed to offer some reassurance for the future, but in late 1956 his employer Henry Parker became ill and died the following year. Then followed a re-run of the old problem of getting a new job and house, for we still lived in a tied house. Six years previously, I had seen my parent's anguish, pain and desperation in a similar situation. At least now, they were not hampered by a young son to care for. Although I was now earning a wage and the immediate financial pressure was less, they were still facing the worrying prospect of being jobless and homeless at the very time they were approaching mid-life. On the previous occasion I had felt a strong sense of unfairness and injustice and those feelings were again ignited. I could now add anger to my feelings.

In those days, for most working families the prospect of owning your own home was not even a dream. They had no money and the option was not even on their radar. For my parents it was again to be a tied house or ideally a rented one. It was a straightforward repeat of the experiences of six years previously with my mother paying regular visits to Windermere Urban District Council and once again to no avail. It was a tense time for the family.

Then lady luck smiled on us. Through the network of neighbours, we learned that there was a vacant tenancy in a group of dwellings known as Meadowcroft Cottages about a mile towards Bowness. The cottage had previously been occupied by the Hantom family, the boys of which I counted amongst my friends. My small family struggled financially to make ends meet but, it must have been much more challenging for large families. The Hantoms were the largest family amongst our group comprising David, Elissa, Frank, Katherine, Charles, Stuart and Donald. All of them prospered. David went to art college, Elissa and Katherine trained as nurses, Frank ended up as a marine engineer travelling the world, Charles became a senior solicitor in a Manchester practice which specialised in trade union work, Stuart was an electrical engineer whilst the youngest Donald also became a solicitor and was commissioned in the Army. It is a remarkable record. Various members of the family were quite political and I spent many hours discussing political ideas with Charles and Frank in particular, whilst David was eventually to become a Labour councillor in Windermere.

The cottages had originally been built by 1912 for the owner of Meadowcroft, John Kenworthy, who had built the main house in 1908 with extensive land holdings and attendant employees. The owner had great plans and exotic interests. In these early years he opened a zoo in the complex adjacent to the workers' homes. Those days had long gone and the owner in the 1950s, Hugh P Jones, had downsized both his predecessor's ambitions and the number of workers employed on his estate. The big house itself was extensively used as a religious retreat for members of evangelical churches.

Mam and Dad knew the key local employee, Eddie Wilkinson, and immediately contacted him. Without ado, he arranged an interview with Mr Jones, the result of which was we were offered the tenancy of 2 Meadowcroft Cottages. Our new home was a terrace house in a block with only one down side that we had to leave our home comforts to go to the outside toilet. This however, was a small price to pay for my parents to obtain one of their lifetime ambitions, a rented house. At long last they had broken out of the vicious cycle of the tied house system. As long as they paid the rent, they had security of tenure. It was heaven to them. They simply couldn't have wished for more.

Having acquired a rented cottage, Dad had the opportunity to free himself completely of the 'big house syndrome' and did so. He decided against working for a single employer but rather to go it alone as a jobbing gardener. This meant he would seek to work for different people in their gardens. This offered new challenges of looking after each garden through all the seasons and doing so with a long-term perspective. It was subtly different from what he had been used to all his life. To put it bluntly he had grown tired being at the whim of any single employer.

With his reputation as a hardworking and knowledgeable gardener, he had no difficulty in getting sufficient hours to fill his working week, including two days a week at Garden Hill whose new owners wanted him to spend even more hours with them but he had decided against. To begin with all went well during the summer months with the long hours of daylight and better weather. Problems began with the onset of winter when the frosty and rainy weather stopped him working and if you didn't work you didn't get paid. It was as simple as that – no work, no pay.

The rain was the main problem. The Lake District has a much higher than the average rainfall in England, often 70 or 80 inches a year – on occasions, it exceeded 100 inches. It was a common sight to see an outdoor worker struggling in the rain with a hessian sack over his shoulders in the forlorn hope of gaining some protection (in those days it was almost exclusively a male preserve). Dad would work in the wet weather if he could. But some tasks such as grass cutting were simply impossible in the rain in the days before the invention of the flymo. On other occasions a hard frost or snow would put paid to him continuing to work.

Repeatedly he would come home on his bike soaked to the skin and then the challenge was to get his clothes dry for the following day, not an easy task in days before central heating and in a cold house. The garments were left hanging over chair backs in the living room where the heat from the dying embers helped with the drying overnight but left a heady aroma of drying gabardine. Another problem was the very nature of the clothes for these were the days before Gore-Tex or even simple waterproof clothing with most raincoats being of gabardine which generally seemed to absorb more rain that they repelled. The most effective waterproof garments came from the military and it was to the military surplus stores, of which there were many in the post-war period, to which you turned for what limited protection was available. These garments were mainly of oilskin and were somewhat cumbersome to work in but they were the best on the market although by modern standards were somewhat ineffective.

Although my dad made a living, the amount was heavily dependent upon the vagaries of the weather. Of course, when he had worked in a 'big house' the weather was the same but then he could manage the work somewhat by keeping back selected indoor jobs, such potting-up or greenhouse work, for a rainy day. He may have been his own boss as a jobbing gardener but he did not have as much control over the work, thus his income was irregular. He enjoyed the variety of work in his new role but worried about the variations in his weekly wage. This was a common worry and Ted Shorrock, who had worked as jobbing gardener prior to Dad, eventually left the profession and took a job with the local council to ensure a regular wage.

But we were happy living at Meadowcroft Cottages. We had known most of the neighbours before moving and got on with them all. That was especially the case with the Shorrock family who lived at number six. Roy was one of my closest friends. His father Ted was a long-time colleague of Dad and his mother, Marjorie, and Mam had known each other for many years. He had a younger brother, John, whom I came to know. John became an apprentice electrician, based at a shop in Bowness and after qualifying and gaining experience, eventually formed his own building company. He prospered although, given the high price of houses, like most other local young people, he had to move to the other side of Kendal. At Meadowcroft, each house in the complex had its own garden laid out in an allotment pattern so Dad was able to continue to supply the family with fresh vegetables. The key factor in their contentment however was knowing they were free from the tyranny of the tied cottage system.

Then one day, out of the blue, a calamity occurred. Ironically my father was working at his old workplace of Garden Hill constructing a new rockery when a piece of slatey rock flew off into one of his eyes. He was rushed to the general practitioner in Bowness who had him transferred immediately to Lancaster Royal Infirmary. For a while the situation looked very serious as it was feared he might lose the eye or even his sight but thankfully the surgeons successfully averted the crisis.

He was kept in hospital under observation for a couple of weeks and by chance he struck up a friendship with Fred Gresswell in the adjacent bed. His new friend was an enthusiastic gardener and they very much enjoyed each other's company. Although he had come from a poor background in rural Lincolnshire he had gone on to be a successful businessman. His parents had run a smallholding on which he began his working life. When he finished fighting in the First World War, he gave up working on the farm, moved away from home and went on to make a fortune in the housing market.

Fred Gresswell lived in a large house, Birklands, at Hest Bank, a village on Morecambe Bay, and as chance would have it, was on the lookout for a fulltime gardener. He had been greatly impressed by Dad's knowledge and general disposition and offered him the job. Following his discharge from hospital, Mam and he discussed

Bowness Bay, 1956, left to right, John Willan, David Clark, Mel Jeffrey and Frank Hanton.

the offer at length, for the accident had brought home to them the precarious nature of jobbing gardening. At that time, he had been without wages for several weeks and faced the prospect that it might be some time before he could work again.

Eventually, my parents decided to leave Windermere which they both loved so much and accept the job thirty miles to the south. They were also very hesitant because of the housing arrangement and my father had already indicated their reluctance on account of this. From his own background, Fred Gresswell fully understood their concerns. Luckily one of his positions was president of the Bradford and Bingley Building Society and he felt sure he could make some alternative arrangement for my parents. After a short while, they decided they trusted Fred and took him at his word. On his assurances, they moved into a house he supplied next to the local railway station, with the West Coast mainline running just a few yards from their back door. When the trains flew past, the house would rattle from cellar to attic. The view from the upstairs was spectacular however, looking across Morecambe Bay to the mountains of Cumbria. During the war they had looked at, and yearned for, the Lakeland hills from the north. They now viewed the same mountains from the south.

It was somewhat ironic that, having escaped the evil of the tied-cottage system, they should give up their independence in a rented house. But their understanding with Mr Gresswell reached a very satisfactory conclusion which eventually enabled them to buy their own small bungalow in Thorns Avenue in the village. The accident which hospitalised Dad, coupled with the days without any wages shook him. He was getting on for sixty and the years of hard physical work were catching up on him.

The move to Hest Bank, away from their beloved Lake District, allowed them to achieve what had seemed an impossible dream for all their lives, the ownership of their own home. It had always seemed an impossibility not only for them but for the overwhelming majority of working people. Finally, they had broken away from the tyranny of the tied house syndrome completely and felt free at last. They had trusted their new boss and their judgement had been rewarded. For the first time in their married lives, they were truly free people. They had shaken off the unfairness of the 'big house' and the oppression of the tied house at one stroke. To say they felt like king and queen would have been no exaggeration. I learned then what freedom can really mean and determined to achieve it myself.

Gone were the years of fear of being made homeless and the terrible feeling of helplessness when it happened. Being completely at the beck and call of every whim of the boss at the 'big house' had taken its toll on Dad. That independence and confidence of the young apprentice at Lowther in 1918 in risking the ire and anger of Lord Lonsdale by joining the local branch of the Agricultural Workers Union had waned over the years. The prospect of knowing that if he lost his job it would mean he would lose the roof over his family's heads, inevitably forced a change in him. His radical feelings were still there but had been subordinated.

Thanks to a benign and generous employer, Fred Gresswell, they gained their freedom in Hest Bank within sight of their beloved Cumbrian Fells.

14

A Village Lost

As I look back from 2020 and living in nearby Windermere, my thoughts turn to the changes in the village of Bowness in which I grew up over seventy years ago. Mam and Dad had moved there in the early 1920s almost a century ago. The changes are massive and I doubt whether my dead parents would recognise the village if they were to return. It is a very different place. Change over time however, is inevitable and over the twentieth century there was gradual change. But the pace of change has speeded up and it has been much more fundamental over the past 25 years than in the previous hundred.

Nowadays, the Windermere Town Council encompasses Bowness, Windermere and the surrounding area. Windermere itself is still a living village but I am afraid is fighting a brave and possibly losing battle. Of my old Bowness school friends who still remain in the immediate area most live in Windermere. I too have chosen to do so on my return to Lakeland. Most of my post-war contemporaries have moved away from the immediate locality where they were brought up. Lack of employment opportunities and especially the price of houses in Bowness have played a part. This has affected the balance of population between the two villages:

In 1931, the population of Windermere Urban District was 6083, comprised of 3772 in Bowness and 2311 in Windermere.

In 1951, the overall figure had increased slightly to 6315, with Bowness falling to 3345 whilst Windermere grew to 2970.

By 2011, the population had increased to 8366, with Bowness increasing to 4041, with Windermere having 4325 residents.

Seventy years ago, there were two villages of Bowness and Windermere, each with vibrant communities and with considerable local rivalry. Although there is a formal divide between them along the Mill Beck which eventually flows into the lake, the most recognisable boundary is Baddeley Clock at the junction of Lake Road and New Road. This clock, facing down towards Bowness, was erected in 1907 in memory of the writer of guide books promoting the Lake

District, M J B Baddeley. It stands in a commanding position immediately in front of where a tank had been positioned during the First World War as a fund-raising initiative. When a youngster, I always felt the clock was huge but now I'm somewhat disappointed by how small it actually is.

As a young boy I rarely went to Windermere unless to catch a bus to Kendal or to go to the village Picture House. I did not even know any young people from Windermere until I went to the secondary school which by then had been relocated further north and more centrally between the two villages on Prince's Road. After 400 years in Bowness, many believe it is now situated in Windermere but it still technically remains in its village of origin. When at school we initially stuck together as Bowness boys but gradually the rivalry diminished. John Hiley, the son of the former teacher, who attended the school ten years after me under a different headmaster, confirmed that in his time at Windermere Grammar School there was still some rivalry between pupils. As someone from Windermere his first allegiance was to fellow pupils from that village and then a pecking order of those from Bowness, Ambleside and finally Staveley.

Although the people of Bowness and Windermere socialised very little together, in the school things were beginning to change. In the 1950s the rivalry between the two villages was nothing new but things were slowly changing. Within a couple of years at Windermere Grammar School friendships between pupils developed and I recall getting to know Len Hayton from the remote Kentmere Valley and Sep Cooper, Iain Johnston and others from Windermere. It was a shift after many years of mistrust and suspicion.

An early example of this liaison between boys of the two villages came when a craze developed for train-spotting. We would cycle up to Cuckoo Bridge on Thwaites Lane to join the Windermere boys watching the trains going in and out of the station. Going onto the station meant buying a platform ticket and why do so when we could watch for free? The engines hauling the trains entering Windermere were quite limited. The majority were those we called 'tankies' which ran to and from Oxenholme and also doubled up as 'bankers' to help main line trains tackle Shap Fell. This interest may not have been long lasting but was an early example of youngsters from the two villages playing together.

Edie Raven who was born in the early years of the last century

(1913) and lived in North Terrace, Bowness, recalled in an unpublished manuscript of her early experiences: "It used to be a nightmare to go to Windermere. No buses then and when you got to the clock (Baddeley) the Windermere gang would be waiting chanting, 'Bowness Boys have no lugs. Poor little devils live in jugs'."

From David and Margaret Richardson, I heard of the same chant with the village names being reversed. I recalled in the 1950s that any football game between the villages at Braithwaite Fold on the outskirts of Bowness, led to much rivalry, some animosity and many spectators. The matches weren't for the fainthearted.

Fifty years earlier Edie Raven remembered similar matches: "When there was the football game between Bowness and Windermere there was some rivalry. The town band used to be out and bring the winning team up the village playing, *See the Conquering Heroes Come.*"

This does not happen now as the two teams have merged, and moved to Queens Park, becoming Windermere AFC. After years of intense rivalry, Bowness Rovers, with decades of success couldn't carry on. Now well into the twenty-first century, many local supporters simply aren't aware of the years of such intense rivalry. In sport, as well as other activities, it isn't unusual for the competition to be most intense the closer the places are.

Over the years this rivalry did die down as the two villages developed different characteristics. Windermere built many more council houses before the Second World War, the 'White City' as it was dubbed by the locals. This was popular and, following the war and the demolition of the prefab houses in Troutbeck Bridge, the local council embarked on an even more ambitious, council house building programme at Droomer, primarily but not exclusively to rehouse the families who had previously lived in the prefabs. This had an effect politically for as late as the mid-1970s, Windermere was one of Labour's stronger areas in South Lakeland. A few years later, a number of social houses were built in an effort to provide more housing for local people. These developments were a key explanation for the growth of Windermere.

In the post war years when I was growing up, behind this apparent uniformity of the twin villages, there were other, quite specific differences amongst the residents. There was some distinction between those who lived on the village outskirts and those who lived in the village itself. We had many things in common; we went to the same junior school, attended the village's parish church, were active in its youth fellowship and of course played and mixed together. I may have lived in the countryside but the village was my hub. This was also the case for my parents.

Nevertheless, my family and others like us had a different lifestyle. We were much more affected by simply living in the countryside. We were more concerned with the weather and the changing seasons. Many of our parents' jobs depended on the land surrounding our homes and of course our homes often depended upon keeping those jobs. In day to day living, distances and transport were major issues and there was simply no slipping out to the shops if we ran short of anything; perhaps nothing dramatic but different. Fortunately in spite of this we were fully accepted by Bowness folk.

Furthermore, just outside the village, notably in the Storrs area, there lived a number of exceedingly rich people. Most were retired successful businessmen from Lancashire and Yorkshire whose beautiful large houses had wonderful views. They passed us on the roads in their fine cars, occasionally splashing us as they did so. A few still maintained their business connections in south Lancashire and largely for their convenience, a direct rail service ran from Windermere to Manchester with a link to Liverpool. The train left at 8.10 in the morning arriving in time for them to get to their offices shortly after 10.15. Then, in the early evening, there was a return train which carried a 'club car' where the same businessmen could relax on their journeys home. The railway company initiated this facility as early as the 1870s and it was still run by British Rail in the 1960s.

People have questioned whether there was resentment between the 'haves' and 'have nots'. I don't recollect that being the case. We may have railed against the tied house system which they controlled, but there was little personal ill-feeling. They were different and few in number. I guess there were less than a hundred such large houses in the area. No, we weren't envious, we were relatively happy with our lives and did not blame them for the wrongs around us which needed correcting. We rarely came into contact with these rich individuals except possibly in a master/servant type of relationship. We had little to do with them and never mixed socially for they played little or no part in village societies.

Admittedly, those from the 'big houses' were prominent in certain exclusive local organisations but locals were rarely permitted to join these bodies in the 1940s and 1950s. In truth, they lived in a parallel universe – a race apart. The Royal Windermere Yacht Club and the Windermere Golf Club were bastions of privilege until more recent times and jealously restricted their membership to those from the higher social groups. Very few local residents were allowed to join even if they could afford to do so.

The Royal Windermere Yacht Club is the most prestigious body with magnificent premises fronting Bowness Bay right in the heart of the village. It was founded in 1860 and has regulated yacht racing on the lake ever since. In 1887, on the Diamond Jubilee of Queen Victoria, it was awarded the Royal Warrant. For many years, one had to hold a certain social status to be a member. Individuals who helped crew the yachts were deemed unsuitable for membership as they were judged as undertaking a servant type role. In essence, they were seen as being from the lower orders. Things have changed. The club is much more liberal in accepting members from a wider background as well as making its premises available to worthy charities. Families, who in past days supplied their products through the club's back doors, are now welcomed as members and some play a prominent role in the organisation.

Whilst not quite so grand, Windermere Golf Club, which is situated in idyllic countryside on the outskirts of Bowness, was formed in 1891 by professional men including clergymen and doctors. The *Golf Monthly*, described the course as "a joyous layout of meandering becks, sweeping descents, strenuous ascents, rocky outcrops, and swathes of luxuriant heather…" Little wonder it attracted members and could be a 'bit choosy' about its membership and for many years restricted its membership largely on social grounds.

It was made clear that tradesmen would not be allowed to become members and this included the prosperous and successful Pattinson family who had built the railway station at Windermere as well as many of the large luxurious houses in the area. The family was so frustrated by their rejection that they built their own golf course much nearer the centre of Windermere village between Beemire Lane and Birthwaite Road. Years later, Cooper Pattinson was so proud of the initiative that he retained a plan of the course in his office. During the Second World War it was converted into allotments helping the 'Dig for Victory Campaign' and was never reconstituted as a golf course. Membership of the Windermere Golf Club is now open. Many locals have joined. Its club house is also offered to charities for fund raising. Mel Jeffrey is a long-time active member, including a period as captain.

Strolling through Bowness today, it is hard to imagine what it was like in my boyhood. Then it provided everything we needed; work, social activity, entertainment, medical services and shops. You could get almost anything you might need and it wasn't necessary to leave the village and most of us didn't, with the exception of an occasional visit to our local market town of Kendal.

In the 1940s and 1950s, there were over 100 shops in Bowness alone. Shops which provided for the needs of local people in every respect with the numbers and type of shops having changed little over the previous fifty years. Many even remained under the same ownership. The shopkeepers by and large accepted their responsibility to meet the needs of the locals who were the means by which they made their living. In turn the shopkeepers were themselves locals and important members of the community.

I recall the village being self-sufficient for all our basic needs and it was generally acknowledged that you hadn't to go far to get everything you required. Even this however, was given a new twist by a life-long resident and owner of the shoe shop in Lake Road, Colin Tyson, who surprised me by explaining: "It was better than that. If you lived in the top of the village you could get all you needed from the shops in the top end. You had no need to visit the bottom of the village for shopping. It was all there near your home."

That really made me realise the significance of the diversity and positioning of the shops. For locals living in different parts of the village, it was more important than I had appreciated. At least it avoided having to carry heavy shopping bags any distance back to your home. In these days, people shopped frequently for they didn't have the storage facilities that we now take for granted. There were no fridges and freezers. Most houses had a pantry, often with a cold slab, which tended to be cooler and it was there that food was kept. It was however, an inefficient means of doing so compared with a fridge. Frequent shopping trips were the solution of villagers. Those living in the countryside without easy access to the shops, just had to rely on their pantry, inefficient as it was. My family's needs were met in the bottom of the village from the top of Crag Brow downwards which was nearer to where we lived and had easier access to the bus.

With the help of David and Margaret Richardson, Colin and

Shops, top of Bowness in 1950s.
Photograph courtesy of Colin Tyson.

Margaret Tyson and Ernie Fallowfield, I was able to compile a list
of shops for the 1950s which I could compare with those existing
in early 2019. John L Campbell, in his scholarly book, *The Village
by the Water,* also provides a list of shops in the 1950s which has
been of considerable help. With the assistance of Edie Raven's list,
it was also possible to see which shops were there in the earlier
twentieth century. The analysis is very revealing and graphically
shows how the village has changed over the previous seventy years
and how it has ceased to service the needs of local people. It is sad
but the easy profits from relentless tourism have destroyed a living
village.

In the 1950s Bowness had:
6 grocery shops, today only the Co-op remains plus a more
    recent Tesco small convenience store.
4 butchers, today there are none.
4 banks, today there are none.
2 fishmongers, today there are none.
2 shoe shops with repairing facilities, today there are none.
2 ironmongers, today there are none.

2 chemists, today there are none.

2 cycle shops, today there are none.

6 sweet shops, the villagers had a sweet tooth.

5 tobacco shops, smoking was still widespread.

3 ladies' hairdressers.

3 gentlemen's hairdressers.

7 ladies' clothing shops.

2 gentlemen's clothing shops.

3 furniture shops.

In the post-war years it was customary for country people when they went into the village shopping to pop into a café for a cup of tea – usually not coffee. Not only did it pass the time until the bus arrived but you could catch up with gossip over a relaxing drink. In those days there were nine cafés in the village with half catering almost entirely for local people as they were a little distance away from the traditional tourist routes. Most of the customers were women for they did the shopping and the gossip would be recounted later to their families at home. It was an established tradition and an integral part of the social scene.

The shops were also crucial in providing jobs. Each shop would provide work for one or two assistants. Tyson's shoe shop not only provided two jobs in sales but a further four jobs repairing shoes. In those days, shoes were initially more expensive in relative terms but could, and would, be repeatedly repaired. We did not live in a throw-away society as we do nowadays. It is easy to see how many, essential local jobs were provided by the shops, all helping to create a cohesive social society based around the village.

By 2020 the number of village shops had increased to over 140 but they were decidedly different in type from those of the 1950s. Shops which met the day to day needs of local people have disappeared to be replaced by those selling non-essential goods. The most dramatic change has been the emergence of no less than 55 cafes or food outlets which amounts to approximately 40% of the total.

Among shops selling essentials, only the Co-op remains as a fully stocked grocery store supplemented by the more recent addition of a small Tesco convenience outlet. Almost all the other shops providing essentials for residents have gone. The emphasis now is to satisfy the tourists. Not all the shops tend to survive for long periods but chop and change according to market forces.

Shops opposite the church in centre of Bowness, 1950s.
Photograph courtesy of Colin Tyson.

In early 2020, Bowness has:
  6 outdoor clothing shops.
  6 gift shops.
  6 toyshops.
  5 shops selling pictures.
  5 beauticians.
  5 women's clothing/fashion shops.
  4 jewellers.
  4 arts and craft shops.
  3 sweet shops.

The remainder include a florist, a wine shop, men's clothes, gents and women's hairdressers, a couple of charity shops as well as sundry other outlets.

These changes are not just because of tourism. There was a strong tourist trade seventy years ago but it was much more seasonal. The shops in those days may have met some of the demands of the visitors but first and foremost served the local residents. The current balance of shops essentially meets the needs of visitors resulting in original residents being driven away from the village. If they remained in the locality many moved to Windermere where their needs are still met by the retailers. There are signs however that Windermere is under pressure as the local tourist industry sets its sights on the village.

Indications of how serious the position had become in Bowness, came in 2014 when it was announced that the Discharged and Demobilised Soldiers and Sailors Club in North Terrace was to close. After over a century, the chairman, Peter Lever, told me that there were insufficient new members coming forward to keep the club sustainable. A sensible arrangement was found and it merged with Windermere Social Club in New Road. It was a symbolic loss to the village. Generations of Bowness men had gone to 'The Club' but now it has been lost. It is a true sign of the irreversible change in the social composition of the village.

Another loss came slightly earlier in the twenty-first century, when St Martin's Church were forced to sell the Parish Rooms on Rayrigg Road to the Old Laundry Theatre. These rooms had been crucial to the life of the village since their opening in 1907 and seventy years previously were central to our social activities – another example of the changing nature of the village.

The Parish Church has suffered further from tourist pressure as a result of problems with parking. Several churchgoers now go to neighbouring local churches where they can park their cars. It is particularly difficult for local parishioners in Bowness where on-street parking is restricted to one hour.

Meanwhile, the changes in the population of Bowness have had a considerable effect on the surrounding area. The dependence on tourism has led to a dramatic decline in the previously robust farming industry. The traditional mixed farming underpinned by the dairy sector which had served the locality well for decades, has come under pressure from the import of milk from other parts of Britain and the European Community. Some farm buildings risked falling into disrepair and dilapidation. Fortunately, the beauty of the landscape has attracted new faces and fresh capital but hidden dangers remain.

At Rosthwaite, Ken and Joyce Scowcroft purchased the farm house and buildings and set about sympathetically restoring and rebuilding it. Without doubt the farm would not have been viable as a free-standing farm and would have inevitably become derelict. Now the dwelling house and former farm buildings are an attractive home with the adjacent fields and fell grazed by Highland cattle, goats, sheep and horses.

Bellman Ground was adjacent but more accessible and in the post war years was a relatively prosperous and successful farm where I spent many hours helping the farmer, Jack Ellis, is no longer a farm. The shippens into which I helped drive the cows for milking, the styes where the pigs grunted happily and the byres where the mother cows waited to calve, are now gone. It belongs to a bygone age. All that is left of the old working farm is the resplendent farmhouse, protected as a Grade II listed building. The farm buildings have found a new use and been converted into attractive dwelling houses which are much in demand. Although I sometimes wonder in my mind whether the current occupants ever hear the lowing of the cows in their ghostlike moments.

Other pressures have affected the farming landscape. It wasn't only the market that hastened the decline of the farming industry, Windermere Urban District Council and later the South Lakeland District Council have intervened, not always helpfully.

Even Rectory Farm which was the nearest farm to the centre of Bowness, was not immune to these pressures and over time became non-viable. It was adjacent to the rectory which was one of the oldest buildings in the vicinity dating back to 1415 and partly rebuilt in 1650. In the early 1950s it was farmed by Jim and Dora Hoggarth, who had two children, Colin and Joyce with whom I occasionally played becoming familiar with the farm. The farm had some particularly good land running down towards the lake but its small size meant it was always a struggle for the family to make a decent living from it. Its viability depended upon obtaining outlying fields for extra grazing. Jim died at the relatively young age of 55. Ironically its very proximity to the tourist attractions turned out to be its downfall.

On the lake the number of boats increased so that those owned by visitors outnumbered those of local people. The council was instrumental in increasing the number of moorings which coincidentally proved to be a lucrative source of money. Over time, there was pressure from those with moorings for boat storage on dry land during the inclement winter months. The council acquired land from the Rectory Farm on which boats could be left over the winter. Next there was a growing demand for visitors' car parking and in turn additional land was taken from the farm. Some of the best farm land was lost to hardstanding for boats and cars.

The local football pitch of Bowness Rovers went the same way. Where I and local lads had spent many happy hours kicking a ball around, there is now a large car park and storage for expensive yachts. The community asset of a green pasture used for local sport for generations has become hard standing for the visitors' cars. In a sense it epitomises the changes in Bowness over the previous half century. The farm itself was never large and the loss of this land meant that the farm became unviable.

At first glance these changes appear to have taken place with no cost to the environment but closer examination shows that subtle and serious changes may be taking place. Already we are witnessing changes in certain bird populations. One of the most common species, the house sparrow or 'spuggie' as we called it, is seen far less. Quite simply it was so common because there was an abundance of food. It relished the husks of corn which were so widely scattered around on all the small mixed farms which were prevalent in the area. Now however there are no such farms. No farms, no grains of corn lying about on which the sparrows can feed – no spuggies.

On the other hand, whereas seventy years ago, Canada and Greylag Geese were rarely seen, nowadays especially near to the lake there are often flocks of up to a hundred strong, feeding on the lush fields which in days past provided sustenance to the herds of milk cattle of Ayrshire, Friesian or Shorthorn cows or during the season were the best hayfields. The landowners and farmers ensured geese didn't come in such numbers for they devoured too much grass which was needed for the cows. It is estimated that each goose can eat 1.8 kilos of grass a day. Thus, a flock of 100 geese would eat sufficient grass to feed up to a dozen cows. Seventy years ago, the farmers would not allow the geese on their fields. To exacerbate the problem, on average a goose deposits nearly a kilo of faecal droppings a day which can transmit diseases to humans. With the geese being largely either near to the lake or on it, the problems need careful monitoring.

The farmers themselves were the best custodians of these matters but they have largely disappeared and with them the care of the land and soil as well as the animals. For a period in the post-war years lime was spread on the fields to counter the naturally acidic soil. To retain the quality of the grass, cow muck which had been collected from the byres was spread over the fields. An early example of recycling but it no longer happens in the fields south of Bowness. Sheep are still around but in recent years I cannot recall seeing a single cow in the fields surrounding Bowness except Highland cattle on Rosthwaite Lot or the odd beef steer.

This lack of care is leading to a deterioration in soil quality. No longer is there proper drainage to ensure the best grass can flourish. Any improvement depends on careful farming. That doesn't exist in the way it did. The hayfield in front of Storrs Hall Hotel, on which Alan Rayner strove so hard to produce good hay, is now almost all covered in reeds and rushes. This trend is beginning to be seen elsewhere in the area. Right across the district an increasing number of good fields are reverting to rushes. I understand this rewilding has positive implications for certain aspects of environmental diversification but unless carefully monitored there could be downsides. Our stone walls are an integral part of our landscape. What happens if they begin to fall down and are not rebuilt? I have seen where this has happened in the Yorkshire Pennines and it is not a pretty sight. In the past the farmers ensured this did not happen. What happens if there are no longer farmers?

Further south at Hill of Oaks, some years ago, the fields ceased to be comprehensively farmed. Now brambles and scrub are taking over with the grass receding inexorably yard by yard. If managed woodlands were being created, this could be welcomed but this is not what is happening.

This is all occurring within the Lake District National Park and in the World Heritage Site which some of us fought for over thirty years to attain. Following our ultimate success, the UNESCO experts and advisors were very clear that the beauty of the Lake District was not natural but was a man made, cultural landscape. It was the sheep farmers who cleared scrub trees on the higher fells on which their animals could graze which in turn produced the mile upon mile of open fell tops which provides so much joy and inspiration today. In the valleys, trees were planted and nurtured, especially in the area around the lake. Then small mixed farms were carved out amongst the trees and the lower fells were added where the sheep and cattle could graze. They became viable cohesive farmsteads which served well both the population and the environment.

In short, what we see and love is shaped by the hand of man. When management patterns change it behoves us to ensure that the beautiful environment we have inherited is safe for people and for the natural world. The Cumbria Wildlife Trust have calculated that the habitat of species-rich grasslands and wildflower meadows in the county has declined by over 97% in the past 50 years. These habitats are crucial for animals, birds, insects and of course flora. Their loss cannot be tolerated. Thankfully some local farmers are planning to create new wildlife meadows.

That applies to the lake itself which was given to the people of Windermere and is looked after on their behalf by the local council and the National Park. The lake at Windermere is a public right of way, which seventy years ago, was rich in flora and fauna. We have seen many of the reed beds, so vital to the natural environment, simply disappear. The explanation was that the wash from speeding motor boats was responsible and thus the Lake District National Park bravely decided that there needed to be a speed restriction on the lake. They prevailed against much opposition from vested interests but have been proved correct by their actions. Some of the reed beds are slowly recovering and the rare char fish are spawning again in the shallow waters where the becks enter the lake. The loud drone of speeding motor boats which was so alien to a national park have also thankfully disappeared.

Other challenges remain for example monitoring the faecal deposits of the geese and at the same time checking for traces of human faeces following the explosion of planning permission for boat houses now used as holiday lets. Traditionally it had been accepted that boathouses would not offer overnight facilities but of late that seems to have gone by the board. Closer monitoring is needed of the increased number of boats which provide overnight accommodation. Those bathing in the lake do need reassurance that it is safe as well as enjoyable.

The council were facing a difficult situation. With the expansion of car ownership combined with a decline in public transport, visitors increasingly arrived in cars with the accompanying need for parking places. With the benefit of hindsight, it marks an early example of the dominance of the tourist industry over community interest. It is legitimate to ask whether it is ever right to entirely sacrifice the local community in preference to possible economic benefit of the few.

The village of Bowness supported a vibrant population for generations. It provided services, employment and shops for the surrounding district – the workers, young people and families like my own who lived there. Today it is captive to a massive tourist industry. That should have been managed much better.

However, I am lucky to have seen the village at its best and today still appreciate living in one of the most beautiful parts of the world. I feel it a real privilege to be able to share that beauty with the millions of tourists. I know they get the same pleasure and satisfaction as I do.

Bibliography

Anon, *Windermere Grammar School: A History*, (*Westmorland Gazette*, 1936).

Armstrong B. & W., *The Arts and Crafts Movement in the North West of England*, (Oblong, 2005).

Banks A. J., *H W Schneider of Barrow and Bowness*, (Banks, 1984).

Bates M., *Snagging Turnips and Scaling Muck*, (Helm, 2001).

Bolton M. R. B., *From Clogs and Wellies to Shiny Shoes*, (Hayloft, 2002).

Brydon A. P., *Sidelights on Medieval Windermere*, (Titus Wilson, 1911).

Buckley N. A., *Around Windermere*, (Frith, 2003).

Campbell J. L., *Village by the Water: A History of Bowness*, (Star Hill, 2015).

Crosskill W. E., *First Beginning*, (Highgate, 1987).

Davies-Shiel M., *Water-Power Mills of South Lakeland*, (Hayloft, 2017).

Hall B., *The Royal Windermere Yacht Club 1860-1960*, (Sherratt, 1960).

Haslam S. E., *John Ruskin and the Lakeland Arts Revival 1880-1920*, (Merton, 2004).

Hayton L., *The Collected Tales of a Lakeland Lad*, (Hayton, 2011).

Hayton L., *Rhymes and Recollections of a Lakeland Lad*, (Hayton, 2016).

Hunt I., *Fenty's Album*, (Pinewood, 1975).

Hyde M., *Broad Leys*, (Compass, 2013).

Kissack E., *The Life of Thomas Mawson*, (Kissack, 2006).

Muir P. L., *The Ferry Inn on Windermere*, (Hayloft, 2011).

Nurse Rev E. J., *History of Windermere Parish Church*, (Boynton & Marshall, 1908).

Pattinson G. H., *Pattinsons, Builders of Windermere*, (Privately published, 1973).

Pattinson G. H., *The Great Age of Steam on Windermere*, (Windermere Nautical Trust, 1981).

Pickering A. D., *Windermere. Restoring the Health of England's Largest Lake*, (Freshwater Biological Association, 2001).

Renouf J. & Rob D., *Voices of the Lake District*, (History Press, 2011).

Sinker Rev J., *Memoirs of Rev Canon Stock*, (Johnson & Sons, 1905).

Taylor C. D., *Portrait of Windermere*, (Hale, 1983)

Waymark J., *Thomas Mawson. Life, Gardens and Landscapes*, (Francis Lincoln, 2009).

White D., *The Windermere Ferry*, (Helm, 2002).

Wright H., *Stanley Webb Davies 1894-1978*, (Bookcase, 2006).

Index

Aberdeen, 134

Accrington Stanley, 73

Adams, Stanley, 113

Agricultural Wages Act, 64

Agricultural Workers Union, 2, 158

All Saints Mission, 83

Allen Technical College, 127

Ambleside, 57, 88, 90-91,100, 106, 113, 130, 160

American War of Independence, 6

Anderson, Jock, 33

Aquatic Ltd, 115

Arbigland, 6, 12

Arts and Crafts,13-4, 24, 62-3, 76

Askham, 2

Atkinson, Alan, 89

Atkinson, Harry, 142

Atkinson, Jimmy, 22-3

Atkinson, Margaret, 88

Atkinson's hairdressers, 19

Attenborough, Sir David, 50

Attlee, Clement, 36, 41, 100, 146

Auty, Harold, 101, 104, 110

Baddeley Clock, 159, 161

Baddeley, M. J. B., 160

Barker Knott, 121

Barnardo's, 3

Baronettes, 149

Barrow-in-Furness, 22, 73-4, 90, 119, 127, 130

Barrowby, 86

Barton, C. D., 102, 111

Barton, Richard, MD, 33

BBC, 32-4, 94

Beckett, John, x, 27, 127, 129

Beeching Report, 137

Beemire Lane, 163

Belfast, 134

Belgium, 135, 142

Belle Isle, 61

Bellman Ground, 118-9, 168

Birklands, 156

Birthwaite Road, 163

Blackbeck Wood, 21, 24, 47, 141

Blacketts, 6

Blackpool, 44

Blackwell House, 62-3

Blair, Tony, 143

Blake Holme Farm, 113, 116

Bolton, 13

Bolton, M., 96-7, 101

Bond Mini-car, 150

Border Hound Trailing Association, 56

Border Regiment, 2, 141

Borwicks Boatbuilders, 114, 129

Bowness, x, 15-6, 19, 26, 31, 38-9, 44m 48, 57-8, 75-6, 79, 81, 88, 90-1, 104, 113, 123, 125-7, 137-8, 142, 146, 148, 150-1, 153, 160-5, 167-8, 170, 172

Bowness Bay, 157, 163

Bowness Boys School, 14, 21, 25, 101, 160-1

Bowness Promenade, 85, 89, 91, 150

Bowness Rectory, 85-6, 169

Bowness Rovers, 73-4, 161, 169

Boy Scouts, 26, 71, 74-82, 88, 106, 108-10, 113

Bradford and Bingley Building Society, 157

Braithwaite Fold, 73, 161

Braithwaite, Isaac, 126

Brampton, 3

Bramwell Evens, G., 34

Brantfell Road, 19

Brathay Hall, 106

175